'A relevant, topical and highly readable text with very interesting ideas for today's practitioner.'

David Pirie,
BSc, PGDip Herbal Medicine,
M. NIMH, Dip. Aromatherapy,
Lecturer in Herbal Medicine

'The information regarding classification of essential oils and blending approaches is both informative and extensive, and the knowledge contained within this text makes it essential reading for students, practitioners and lecturers of Aromatherapy and indeed other complementary therapies… Dr Jennifer Rhind was an inspiration to me and I know that my copy of her book will never be far from reach.'

Lesley Ann Potter,
BSc Complementary Therapies (Aromatherapy),
Lecturer in Complementary Therapies

'As a student I found Dr Rhind's book easy to use with a wealth of information about a very wide range of oils. The suggestions for therapeutic blending are invaluable. As a practising aromatherapist, *Essential Oils: A Handbook for Aromatherapy Practice* is still my first point of reference.'

Cath Boyle,
MA (Hons) Sociology,
BSc Complementary Therapies
(Aromatherapy), PGCE, MIFPA

Essential Oils

A Handbook for Aromatherapy Practice

Dr Jennifer Rhind

NAPIER UNIVERSITY
EDINBURGH

For my husband, Derek, and Leeloo

This edition published in 2009 by:
Napier University, Edinburgh

Edited, designed and produced by:
BA (Hons) Publishing students:
Catriona Campbell, Ross Coverdale, Rob Jordan,
Laura Kincaid, Kirsten Watt and Leigh Young.
School of Arts and Creative Industries,
Napier University, Edinburgh

Distributed by:
The Faculty of Health, Life and Social Sciences,
Napier University, Edinburgh

A catalogue record for this book is available from the British Library

ISBN: 978-0-9559362-1-0

Printed by:
Bell & Bain Ltd, Glasgow, G46 7UQ

Contents

List of Tables

FOREWORD

In fifteen years of studying aromatherapy, I have rarely found a text that provides essential oil information which is supported by contemporaneous research. Many publications are dated or interpret the actions of essential oils according to the herbal use of plants rather than their chemical structure. In contrast, Jennifer's book is clear, detailed and sequential; information on the approaches to synergistic blending and the therapeutic uses of essential oils is backed up by a wide variety of established references, with direct applications to practice included throughout.

An accomplished academic with a degree in Applied Microbiology and a PhD in Mycotoxicology, Jennifer has dedicated nearly twenty years to the study and practice of complementary therapies, and aromatherapy in particular. Informed by scientific disciplines and strong educational philosophies, her book is a valuable contribution to the field of aromatherapy and provides an excellent reference for students and practitioners alike.

Frances Rawlings, RN (retired),
BEd, MSc Complementary Therapy Studies,
FIFPA Fellow and past Chair of the International
Federation of Professional Aromatherapists

ACKNOWLEDGEMENTS

CONTRIBUTOR

Sue Jenkins, Lecturer, Napier University; 2008 Chair, the International Federation of Professional Aromatherapists.

THANK YOU

Dr Christine Donnelly, Programme Leader, BA (Hons) Complementary Therapies at Napier University, for your unfailing encouragement, never-ending support and keeping me on track.

Thanks also to Howard Wollman and Lizi Irvine of the School of Health and Social Sciences at Napier University for your support.

Dr Lim Lit-Sing (Lawrence), Hong Kong, for inspiration and the sensory journey.

Kareen Hogg, for your support and organisation.

Sue Jenkins, for your contributions and checking of the information.

Sandie New, for your perception, and being there.

Hugh Rooney, for your alternative, energetic perspectives.

Peter Akyeampong, Lecturer and Homeopath, for your thoughtfulness, care and remedies for all occasions.

All my aromatherapy students, past and present.

Special thanks to Derek Allan, Avril Gray and David McCluskey of the BA (Hons) Publishing programme at Napier University and their third-year Publishing students, without whom this book would not have been possible.

Introduction

This handbook has been written to provide a source of unambiguous, accessible information on the essential oils used in contemporary aromatherapy practice, with an emphasis on their therapeutic applications and the underlying philosophical approaches to these applications.

Reliable and referenced information on essential oils underpins sound aromatherapy practice. Essential oils can also be integrated with other bodywork and energy therapies – this is an area that has yet to be fully explored. Therefore this handbook may be a useful resource for other complementary therapy practitioners, for example massage therapists and reflexologists.

Section 1 is an exploration of synergistic blending because, in holistic aromatherapy practice, essential oils are used in combinations rather than singly, in the belief that the therapeutic potential of a blend is greater than the sum of its essential oil components. A range of approaches to blending is examined: Maury's Individual Prescription, which forms the basis of the holistic approach, Franchomme and Pénoël's molecular approach, psycho-olfactory approaches and the Traditional Chinese Medicine (TCM) inspired energetic approaches of Mojay and Holmes.

Section 2 is organised into three sub-sections, based on the botanical classification of essential oil bearing plants and types of aromatic products (differentiating between essential oils and absolutes). This approach encourages better understanding, as often essential oils of the same botanical family will share many characteristics, and discourages learning by rote. The profiles contain relevant information concerning the characteristics of each essential oil that, where possible, informs evidence-based practice without information overload. The profiles also contain information directly applicable to practice, such as blending suggestions, based on the holistic approach.

A comprehensive glossary, an index of the chemical composition of essential oils, a therapeutic index and a list of carrier oils in aromatherapy are provided.

The information is based on reliable texts, journal articles and the experience of the aromatherapy teaching team at Napier University, Edinburgh. The text is referenced throughout. For more detail on each essential oil, the original sources should be consulted.

Section 1

Approaches to Essential Oil Selection and Blending

The holistic approach to aromatherapy treatment includes the synthesis of a synergistic prescription of essential oils for an individual, not simply for a collection of symptoms. As aromatherapy practice has developed, several distinct approaches to selecting and blending essential oils have emerged. The original, holistic approach advocated by Maury (the 'Individual Prescription') remains the method of choice for many aromatherapists.

However, a more clinical approach, used by practitioners of aromatic medicine such as Franchomme and Pénoël, is based on the molecular structure and functions of essential oil constituents. This offers a more scientific way of thinking that is increasingly being adapted for use by aromatherapists. Psycho-olfactory approaches appeal to therapists who adhere to the philosophy that it is the aroma of the essential oils that contributes most significantly to the therapeutic outcomes, while other therapists and writers, such as Mojay and Holmes, advocate an energetic approach, based on TCM principles.

All these approaches are valid. The choice remains with the therapist, based on the needs of the client at the time.

Synergy and Antagonism

> The synergistic rationale for using combination products looks to producing a dynamic product that has multiple modes of action, respecting the principle that the action of the combined product is greater than the sum total of known and unknown chemical components.
>
> (Harris 2002)

In aromatherapy, it is good practice to use synergistic combinations of essential oils; that is, to select and combine essential oils that will support and enhance each individual oil's actions.

Each essential oil will have a range of therapeutic actions and can therefore be indicated for use in many circumstances. However, a particular essential oil can possess a whole array of therapeutic actions that makes it particularly useful in very specific instances. All essential oils may have actions on the physical, physiological and psychological levels but it seems likely that some oils will have more pronounced actions at one (or two) of these levels.

An essential oil is composed of many chemical constituents, each contributing to a greater or lesser extent to the effects of the essential oil. Some constituents will enhance the effects of other constituents; therefore the effect of the whole essential oil is greater than that of its individual chemical components. This is called synergy. For example, two of the main constituents of true lavender oil, linalyl acetate and linalool, are credited with sedative action, and these components work together to give true lavender oil its sedative properties.

Sometimes, constituents in an essential oil may in fact have opposing actions, and the overall effect of the oil will depend on the relative proportions of antagonistic components. For example, rosemary essential oil contains 1,8-cineole and α-pinene. 1,8-cineole has been shown to have spasmolytic effects on tissues, while α-pinene has distinct spasmogenic effects (Buchbauer 1993). Therefore varying extents of spasmolysis can be observed, depending on the 1,8-cineole content of rosemary oil. This in turn depends on the variety, origin and the time that the crop is harvested.

There is some evidence to support the concept of synergy and antagonism in essential oil combinations (Harris 2002). In holistic aromatherapy practice, where endless possibilities for essential oil combinations exist, largely unsupported by any hard evidence, synergy and antagonism within blends are virtually impossible to assess.

Maury's Individual Prescription

In 1961, Marguerite Maury wrote the influential aromatherapy text *Le Capital Jeunesse* which was translated into English in 1964 *(The Secret of Life and Youth)*. Maury's student, Daniel Ryman, instigated the reprint of this seminal work in 1989.

Maury developed the concept of preparing a mixture of aromatic essences based on 'the physiological and psychic identity of the individual'. She called this the 'individual prescription' or IP (Maury 1989). Maury's philosophies were influenced by her studies of Tibetan Medicine.

> The individual mixture is designed to reflect the weaknesses and violence of an individual; it has to compensate for the deficiencies and reduce the excesses. It serves above all to normalise the rhythm of the functions. The latter risk, either by inveigling the body into excessive expenditure of energy or by an over-accentuated slowing down, preventing it from satisfying the demands made on it. For these reasons the individual mixture may be compared to the negative of a film with its reversed shadows and light.
>
> Maury (1989, p. 95)

The individual prescription should be based on as much information about the client as possible, and the aim should always be to restore balance. The physical and physiological condition should be considered in conjunction with the state of mind.

When Maury's examples of IPs are examined, it becomes apparent that, in general, essential oils classed as base notes impact on the physical and cellular level, middle notes affect function and rhythm, and top notes impact on the limbic system. She was adamant that the balance of essences in the mixture was very important. During a course of aromatherapy treatments, Maury would modify the blend when appropriate.

> We should like to point out that an IP is only correct and effective when it has become a combination and has not merely remained a simple mixture.
>
> Maury (1989, p. 100)

In the light of modern aromatherapy practice, this concept can be adapted and used. Today, in holistic aromatherapy practice, therapists do not adhere rigidly to the recommended inclusion of top, middle and base notes in every blend, and the choice of essential oils is more often based on knowledge of their potential therapeutic actions.

However, the combination of the oils remains important, as does the holistic assessment of the client's physical, physiological and psychological needs on each occasion. So, Maury's philosophies have become embedded in current practices.

Holistic Intent

If a blend is prepared to suit the holistic profile of the individual, the following must be given equal importance:

- physical signs and symptoms
- areas or body systems that are not functioning optimally
- areas and body systems that are currently affected by stress, diet and lifestyle
- areas or systems that may be subject to future dysfunction (hereditary weaknesses or lifestyle implications)
- emotional and behavioural signs and symptoms, coping mechanisms

The above can be identified from the client's history and from close observation. In some cases, the therapist may need to prioritise these factors; however none should be overlooked. The aims and direction of the blend need to be clear, and the overall balance of the blend should be tailored to suit the individual.

The therapist, in conjunction with the client, needs to establish what physical and physiological signs, symptoms or factors are causing most concern, and which body systems are 'out of balance'. A list of essential oils that could support these systems and help redress balance can be made. Generally, it will be possible to identify one or two oils that are indicated strongly for the individual.

The client's emotional state must also be considered – what emotional/behavioural signs and symptoms have become apparent? Potentially helpful oils can be identified, and any strongly indicated oils noted.

The therapist must then decide on the combination. Where possible, the 'shortlisted' oils will be included, unless they could be antagonistic to one another – this would modify the overall effect of the blend. Some of the essential oils that did not make the 'shortlist' can also be included, if they could be viewed as contributing to the desired effects. Based on current knowledge, Harris (2002) has produced some sound guidelines for formulating potentially synergistic blends of essential oils for aromatherapy practice. These are summarised below.

- remain focussed on the purpose of the blend – do not attempt to achieve too many goals within one formula
- select essential oils that are complementary to one another in terms of activity, direction, and chemistry
- restrict the number of essential oils in the blend to between three and seven. If too many essential oils are used in a formula, the active ingredients will be diluted and the dose will be below the therapeutic level
- ensure the final blend remains high in active components
- select the base (carrier) with care as this is also part of the synergy/antagonism issue
- apply at the dose appropriate for the application
- be aware that there will also be a synergistic/antagonistic therapist/client relationship
- the psychological effect of the odour will contribute to or detract from the synergistic potential

- if massage is used as part of the intervention, the psychological, physiological and physical effects of massage will also impact on the treatment outcome

Ultimately, the selection should reflect the individual at the physical/cellular level, the rhythms and balance of his or her body functions, and the psyche – as advocated by Maury.

The Molecular Approach

This approach to synergistic blending is based on the 'functional group' hypothesis. Historically, Charabot and DuPont initiated this concept. While investigating fragrance chemistry, it became clear that many of the properties of essential oils, including their odours, could be explained in terms of chemical composition – especially the presence of functional groups on molecules. The pioneers of French medical aromatherapy, Franchomme and Pénoël, applied the same concept (i.e. structure determines function) to help explain the therapeutic properties of essential oils (Schnaubelt 2000). A summary can be found in Table 1 (page 12).

There is little doubt that there is a relationship between the chemical structure of odour molecules and their physiological and pharmacological properties. The influence of functional groups has been linked with rather specific properties and actions. There has been a tendency to over-generalise this concept, and consequently many erroneous assumptions have been made. For example, some ketones such as thujone are neurotoxic, but not all ketones are toxic to the nervous system – especially the low levels found in most essential oils.

However, the functional group hypothesis does provide a useful starting point if it is remembered that ultimately each molecule must be considered as a whole, not just as a functional group, that each essential oil contains many different types of molecules and the whole oil must be considered.

Medical Aromatherapy

Pénoël (1998/1999) identifies that medical aromatherapy, using the 'molecular approach' may have curative purpose, preventative action or even be applied for an evolution search, i.e. 'I feel well, but I want to feel even better and improve my potential in general and/or specific areas.' He also considers that 'aromatic care' can be emergency, intensive or regular, for chronic states. Although the approach to blending is reductionist, the intent can remain holistic.

The molecular approach can be applied in 'Anglo-Saxon' aromatherapy, for constructing potentially synergistic blends. Essential oil blends can be created for either 'horizontal' or 'vertical' synergistic actions (Pénoël 1998/1999). Both approaches have their merits, and they are outlined below.

Horizontal synergy refers to a blend of several essential oils containing similar functional groups for a single specific purpose. For example, an antimicrobial blend of several monoterpene alcohol-rich essential oils such as *Cymbopogon martinii* (geraniol), *Melaleuca alternifolia* (terpinene-4-ol), *Thymus vulgaris* CT (thujanol) and *T. saturoides* (borneol) demonstrates horizontal synergy, where the molecules identified enhance each other's antimicrobial actions.

Table 1
The molecular approach – the influence of functional groups

Chemical group	Effects – general and specific	Examples – specific
Monoterpenes	General tonic and stimulant	
	Decongestant – mucous (exocrine glands)	α- and β-pinenes
	Cancer prevention and treatment	
	Hormone-like properties – action on the pituitary adrenal system – adrenalin production	Limonene
	Analgesic	*Pinus*, Myrcene, para-cymene
Sesquiterpenes	Anti-inflammatory – counter histamic reactions	Chamazulene, β-caryophyllene
	Hormonal effects	Farnesene
Monoterpene alcohols	Antibacterial	
	Vasoconstrictive	
	Local anaesthesia	Menthol
	Tonifying and stimulant	Terpinene-4-ol
	Sedative	Linalool
	Spasmolytic	Linalool
Sesquiterpene alcohols	General tonic (<monoterpene alcohols)	
	Phlebotonic	Viridiflorol, cedrol
	Cardiotonic	Santalol
	Neurotonic	α- and β-eudesmol
	Oestrogenic	Viridiflorol
	Anti-inflammatory	α-bisabolol
	Anti-cancer effects	Farnesol, nerolidol α-bisabolol
	Antiviral	Sanatlenes, santalols
	Antimalarial	Nerolidol

Table 1 (continued)
The molecular approach – the influence of functional groups

Chemical group	Effects – general and specific	Examples – specific
Phenols	Tonics and general stimulants Antimicrobial Analgesic	 Thymol and carvacrol Eugenol
Aldehydes	Calming to CNS Anti-inflammatory Antimicrobial Antifungal	Citral Citral Cinnamaldehyde (aromatic) Citral, cinnamaldehyde
Ketones	Mucolytic Wound healing Antihaematomal Antiviral (papilloma, herpes)	Menthone Italidiones
Esters	Antispasmodic Sedative	Linalyl acetate Esters in Roman chamomile, linalyl acetate
Oxides	Expectorant Antispasmodic	1,8-cineole, linalool oxide
Ethers	Antispasmodic Analgesic Euphoric	
Lactones	Mucolytic Expectorant Analgesic	Alantolactone, isoalantolactone Nepetalactone

From Bowles (2003)

Horizontal synergy would be considered if treating a client with a specific aim in mind, e.g. to treat infection. Although holistic aromatherapists cannot claim or offer to treat a specific disease, the intent of the blend could be to combat infection, the combination could benefit the client in other ways, as each essential oil possesses a spectrum of activity.

Vertical synergy refers to a blend of essential oils containing different functional groups, intended for more than one purpose. For example, an antimicrobial monoterpene alcohol combined with a mucolytic monoterpene ketone and an antispasmodic ester would demonstrate vertical synergy. In this case, essential oils could be *Cymbopogon martinii* (geraniol) with *Mentha piperita* (menthone) and *Lavandula angustifolia* (linalyl acetate) (Pénoël 1998/9).

Vertical synergy is usually more appropriate in holistic aromatherapy practice, where a client presents with more than one requirement. Even a single disease normally entails several different pathophysiological processes. As each essential oil in the blend will contain more than one type of functional group, there is scope for further overlap of properties.

The Molecular Approach Debate

Since the early 1990s, there has been an ongoing debate about the validity of the molecular approach, especially when the concepts are applied to Anglo-Saxon aromatherapy practice.

Schnaubelt (2003) comments on the Franchomme and Pénoël hypothesis that the properties of an essential oil are determined by the functional groups of its constituent molecules.

> If functional group therapy is seen as a rigid dogma (e.g. all aldehydes are sedative), it is self contradictory. I might venture to say that this certainly was not the intent of those who originally put forward this concept. However if functional group therapy is understood as an attempt to understand the physiological effects of essential oils, it certainly contributes to the therapeutic utilisation of essential oils.
>
> Schnaubelt (2003)

He also argues that:

> [O]ne dimensional pharmacology can only do so much to explain its (aromatherapy) benefits. Do we even need this type of research at all if its main purpose is to simply legitimise aromatherapy as a healing modality to mainstream scientific experts? I cannot suppress the notion that the more aromatherapy strives to be accepted by the medical profession, the more it is likely to copy its mistakes and failures.
>
> Schnaubelt (2000)

The molecular approach, when applied to aromatherapy, has indeed a few pitfalls.

Firstly, the majority of the pharmacological actions attributed to essential oil functional groups/molecules (originally in Franchomme and Pénoël's *L'Aromathérapie Exactement*) have not been 'verified' by independent researchers, so the evidence must be regarded as empirical in the meantime.

Secondly, the physiological effects attributed to many essential oil molecules/whole oils are often based on oral/rectal administration, not dermal absorption at the low levels used in aromatherapy. Thus it may not be correct to assume that an approach used in aromatic medicine is equally valid for aromatherapy.

Finally, the essential oils are considered largely in terms of their possible pharmacological actions – giving little or no consideration to the psycho-olfactory influence that is so important in Anglo-Saxon aromatherapy.

> Those who wish to use aromatherapy have to rely on their own observations, experience and experimentation. It may unsettle those loyal to the conventional system, but it is precious and it makes aromatherapy one of the few therapeutic systems truly not tested on animals but on humans.
>
> Schnaubelt (2000)

Psycho-olfactory Approaches

Aromatherapy – Vibrational Medicine?

In 1996, Luca Turin, a biophysicist at University College, London, proposed the 'Vibrational Induced Electron Tunnelling Spectroscope Theory'. Turin claimed that central to the process of olfaction was the frequency at which the bonds of an odorant molecule vibrate (Turin 1996).

He proposed that olfactory receptors are tuned to the vibrational frequency of odours. So perhaps the psycho-olfactory aspect of aromatherapy is due to vibrational energy.

This has an impact on physiology via the nervous system and endocrine system. However, this could also have an impact at an energetic level.

Aromatic Typology

Philippe Mailhebiau (1995) developed the concept of 'caractérologie' of essential oils, linking the olfactory characteristics or 'personalities' of essential oils with the olfactory affinities and temperament of the individual. He uses this concept to refine and personalise his aromatherapy treatments so that they not only address symptoms/complaints, but also aim to restore balance and equilibrium.

In his book, *La Nouvelle Aromathérapie: caractérologie des essences et tempéraments humains* (published in the UK as the abbreviated form *Portraits in Oils*), he explores the idea of aromatic typology and the psycho-sensory impact of essential oils. His approach was intuitive in origin, and has been compared to the work of Hahnemann, the founder of homeopathy (Clerc 1995).

He does maintain throughout that aromatherapy is a specialised medical field; his work is firmly grounded in aromatic medicine, however there is much in his writing that could influence 'psycho-olfactory' blending in aromatherapy. He claims 'from a therapeutic point of view, this approach opens the door to personalised treatments which go beyond the scope of symptomatic aromatherapy by combining efficient physiochemical action with a decisive psychosensory [*sic*] effect' (Mailhebiau 1995).

Sensory Impact of Aromatherapy

Michel Lavabre (1990) has also suggested that the psycho-sensory philosophy should be central to aromatherapy practice. His *Aromatherapy Workbook* (1990) contains some interesting ideas, not least the concept of morphogenetic fields, the Gaia hypothesis and evolution-involution.

Mojay (1996) holds the view that it is the fragrance that has the most immediate and generalised effect on the body and mind. So in aromatherapy it is important to engage directly with essential oils in these terms: experiencing the fragrances of essential oils from roots, stems, leaves, grasses, woods, resins, flowers, fruits and seeds. Remember, because you are connecting directly with the essential oils through their fragrances, you are using your sense of smell, gaining tangible insights into how they act on us. The following theories are influenced by anthroposophy, founded by Rudolph Steiner.

Essential Oils from Roots

Roots anchor a plant to the ground, and water and nutrients enter the plant via its root system. In some plants, the roots also act as an organ of food storage. Ginger, spikenard and vetivert essential oils are obtained from roots. Typically oils from roots have grounding, nurturing and warming qualities. There are times in our lives when we may feel uneasy, insecure, scared or out of touch.

These oils can help us get in touch with our ‘roots’ and feel anchored or grounded. Examples are:

Ginger (from rhizomes) – warming and stimulating

Spikenard – sedative and soothing

Vetivert (from rootlets) – the 'oil of tranquillity'

Essential Oils from Stems and Leaves

The stems and leaves are the aerial parts of the plant – the very obvious, dynamic, living elements. Not only do they form the main structure, they also are where photosynthesis and gas exchange occur. Plants use carbon dioxide as a carbon source and release oxygen into the atmosphere. Many essential oils are obtained from stems and leaves, in some cases the entire aerial parts of a plant, sometimes the leaves and twigs, and sometimes just the flowering tops of herbaceous plants. Essential oils obtained from leaves often have an affinity with the respiratory system. Such oils can be helpful not only with physical problems in this system, e.g. infections, but also on an emotional level, e.g. when we find it difficult to breathe deeply, when it is hard to 'let go' or release feelings which affect our well-being, or when our minds are cluttered and we need mental clarity. Examples include:

Basil (leaves of herb) – cephalic (clears the head)

Eucalyptus blue gum (leaves of tree) – stimulating, cephalic, cooling

Sweet marjora (aerial parts) – sedative and warming

Melissa (aerial parts of herb) – calming and comforting

Peppermint (aerial parts of herb) – refreshing, stimulating and tonic

Essential Oils from Grasses

The types of plants known as grasses belong to a large botanical family called the *Poaceae.* This is a diverse family, whose members are widespread over the earth. These grasses have extensive roots (vetivert is a member of this family), and the aerial parts are characterised by long narrow linear leaves. Grasses are economically an important family, containing the cereals – man's staple diet – however, they are also grown as pasture and animal fodder. A few grasses have aromatic leaves, and are sources of essential oils, such as lemongrass and palmarosa. Their essential oils are useful antimicrobials that are supportive of the immune system. However, they are derived from a family that is in essence about nurturing and they can also strengthen our physiological balance and immune systems by imparting emotional support – their aromas comfort and relieve anxiety. Oils from the grasses are very useful when you are experiencing debility, lethargy or fatigue – both mental and physical. Examples include:

Lemongrass – antidepressant and uplifting

Palmarosa – anxiolytic and calming

Essential Oils from Woods

Some plants such as trees and shrubs have woody stems. Woody tissues are often aromatic and yield a wide range of essential oils. Woody essential oils can be found in a range of botanical families.

The conifers, which are found in colder and temperate climates, yield oils that are typically warming and restorative, perhaps reflecting the characteristics they need to survive. Others, such as those from the Lauraceae and Santalaceae families, grow in tropical and subtropical climates. It is not easy, therefore, to generalise about woody oils, however, like the leaves and stems, woody essential oils often have affinities with the respiratory system. Woody essential oils tend to help the individual find balance and equilibrium – they are good aids to meditation. So if you need to feel centred, and to open your consciousness, they are a good choice. Examples include:

Atlas cedarwood – stimulating, uplifting and anxiolytic

Cypress – restorative, soothing and refreshing

Pine – calm vitality

Rosewood – calming and refreshing

Sandalwood – uplifting and calming

Essential Oils from Resins

Some woody plants produce aromatic resins and gums which have been used in incenses, perfumery and as astringents (controlling secretions from exocrine glands) and healing agents for thousands of years. Some of their oils are used in aromatherapy. Like the woody oils, they are very well suited for times when you need to find your core being and inner peace, perhaps along with meditation or contemplative practice. Examples include:

Benzoin resinoid – comforting, soothing

Frankincense – revitalising

Galbanum – clearing

Myrrh – restoring and uplifting

Essential Oils from Flowers

Flowers are the reproductive parts of the plant. Not all flowers contain enough volatile oil to make extraction a viable process, and even when the oil can be extracted, the yield of essential oils from flowers is usually very low. Often, solvent extraction is the most efficient method – producing an 'absolute'. Echoing the biological role of their source, the flower oils usually have intense, sometimes sensual, aromas, associated with all aspects of creativity.

At times of emotional shock, the flower oils can bring comfort and they can help allay anxieties – especially those related to the social domain such as poor self-image, shyness and lack of confidence. They are useful when you feel that you are lacking imagination or creative drive, or even the urge to have fun, or play, as some have quite pronounced euphoric effects. Examples include:

Roman chamomile – calming and anxiolytic

Jasmine – stimulating, warming, imparts joy and euphoria

Neroli – hypnotic, calming, soothing

Rose – antidepressant, anxiolytic, comforting

Ylang ylang – calming, euphoric

Essential Oils from Fruits and Seeds

Fruits are the structures that develop to protect the seeds that form from the fertilised ovules in flowers. Essential oils can be extracted from different types of fruit, from the small fruits used as spices, to the large citrus fruits, whose peel contains fairly large amounts of volatile oils. In some cases it is the seeds contained within the fruit that are the source of the oil. Fruit and seed oils have an affinity with the digestive system – not just on a physical level but also on a mental level.

All the citrus oils have refreshing odours that will impart happy feelings, while the spicy oils derived either from the seeds or the entire fruits tend to confer the energy contained within their source and have stimulating, revitalising and strengthening effects. As their effects on the digestive system are via reflex action – think of the stimulation of the salivary glands when you smell lime – they can be very useful at the times when you are feeling low and have lost appetite (either for food or life!).

The citrus oils are also described as useful 'detoxifiers' (grapefruit and lemon especially) – and can be useful if you feel that you need to clear out and make a fresh start.

Cardamom – stimulating, refreshing, warming

Citrus – uplifting, antidepressing

Coriander – comforting and revitalising

Sweet fennel – balancing, revitalising, clearing

Black pepper – restorative, strengthening

The suggested effects above are subjective yet commonly reported experiences to the aromas of these essential oils. You may well notice that your perceptions are different, therefore try not to place too much emphasis on personal likes and dislikes, as they are all equally valuable in the therapeutic sense.

Energetic Approaches to Blending

Two authors/practitioners, Gabriel Mojay and Peter Holmes, have pioneered the energetic approach to aromatherapy, using an Eastern frame of reference. The following is a very brief summary of their approaches.

Aromatherapy – for Healing the Spirit

> All essential oils have the power to affect us both emotionally and spiritually. Only those that are right for the individual – at that moment in their life – will possess the subtle potential to transform.
>
> Mojay (1999)

> Fragrance is the primary effective quality of essential oils. By this we mean their most immediate and generalised effect on the body and mind. This effect is first and foremost an energetic effect – as it is the vital energy of the human organism that first responds to an essential oil and its fragrance.
>
> Mojay (1999)

Mojay uses the framework of the Oriental Five Elements to explore the fragrance energies of essential oils, proposing that Five Element Theory allows the therapist to align the actions of essential oils with holistic therapeutic intentions that encompass the body, emotions and spirit (Mojay 1996).

The theory of the Five Elements is central to Traditional Chinese Medicine. The elements are distinct from those of the Western traditions (Fire, Air, Earth and Water) – they are phases or movements of yin and yang energy, manifesting in Fire, Earth, Wood, Metal and Water. Each individual is considered to be a mixture of all five elemental energies and processes. Mojay has begun to explore the fragrance energies of essential oils in relation to their vital therapeutic actions.

If the therapist is able to conduct a holistic assessment of the client in terms of the Five Element Theory, essential oils can then be selected for their energetic properties rather than their pharmacological actions. However, the aromatherapist must also have knowledge of the underpinning theory in order to use this approach.

The attractions of this novel system are numerous. It does not rely on the attributed, but not always substantiated, physical and physiological actions of essential oils. As mentioned, some of these actions may not even be applicable in aromatherapy, because of the mode of administration. In addition, the individual's response to the fragrance of the essential oils is at the core of this approach. Psychological, emotional and behavioural responses to odour have been very well researched and documented (Van Toller and Dodd 1988, Jellinek 1994, Kirk-Smith 1995, Knasko 1997, Torii 1997). From the holistic perspective, this is inextricably linked with the energetic domain.

Fragrance Energetics

Peter Holmes (1997) developed the concept of fragrance energetics, using three fragrance parameters – tone (odour quality), intensity and note (evaporation rate), with tone being the most significant. He identifies six fragrance categories (spicy, sweet, lemony, green, woody and rooty) and proposes that the nature of a fragrance will bring about specific psycho-therapeutic effects.

The following summarises Holmes' suggestions.

> 'High/top tone' oils such as those from the citrus group, the Myrtaceae family e.g. *Eucalyptus*, *Ravensara*, niaouli, also ylang ylang extra and 1, lavender and mimosa abs. will have a stimulating, uplifting effect.
>
> 'Low/base tone' oils including vetivert, patchouli, sandalwood and also tuberose, hay and oakmoss abs., most pine oils, and cinnamon bark will have a depressing, sedating effect.
>
> Spicy oils are stimulating, invigorating, intensifying, awakening, opening and dispersing.
>
> Sweet oils are relaxing, calming, harmonising, regulating, moistening dissolving, nourishing and regenerating.
>
> Lemony oils are clearing, clarifying, sensitising, focusing, energising and invigorating.
>
> Green oils are balancing and regulating, cooling, relaxing, clearing and clarifying.
>
> Woody oils are centring, contracting, grounding and strengthening.

> Rooty oils are stabilising, grounding, solidifying, tonifying, desensitizing and calming.

Each of these energetic odour effects can then be selected to counteract negative mood states. For example, woody essential oils such as sandalwood, which has 'centring' and contracting properties, can be used to help with feelings of insecurity and loss of boundaries. The mechanism of the choice of oils appears to be similar to that of the Bach flower remedies.

Blending Aesthetics

Regardless of the philosophical approach to blending essential oils for aromatherapy, it is vital that the blend is aesthetically pleasing and acceptable to the recipient as well as reflecting their individual needs. If it is not, the synergistic potential will be reduced (Harris 2002), and there will be implications involving the hedonic response (Kirk-Smith 1995) and the placebo effect (Hongratanaworakit & Buchbauer 2007).

The Lavabre Approach to Aesthetic Blending

Lavabre (1990) uses the established concept of perfume notes, in conjunction with his own concept of blend modifiers, enhancers and equalisers. This system can be usefully and successfully applied when creating essential oil blends using any of the blending approaches. Lavabre's ideas are particularly helpful for those new to blending, or who are in the early stages of sensory analysis of essential oils.

Modifiers (or personifiers) are intense fragrances that have a major impact on the fragrance of the blend – even in tiny amounts – and can be found in top, middle and base categories. They give a blend real personality and can be used to improve 'flat' blends. Generally they should be used sparingly to avoid totally dominating a blend. Examples are clove, cinnamon, peppermint, thyme, German and Roman chamomiles and patchouli.

Enhancers also have strong presence, but they are not as overpowering as the modifiers. Consequently, they can be used in greater proportions within a blend than the modifiers. Examples are bergamot, cedarwood, geranium, clary sage, lavender, lemon, lime, may chang, palmarosa, sandalwood, ylang ylang, jasmine, rose, neroli and myrrh.

Equalisers are the essential oils that help improve harsh blends, dampen down unwanted intensity of over dominant notes, fill 'gaps' and help the blend flow. They should not have an effect on the overall personality. Equalisers are context dependant. Lavabre maintains that rosewood and wild Spanish marjoram are universal equalisers. Orange and tangerine can be used with neroli, petitgrain and bergamot, and citrus oils act as equalisers with spice oils such as clove, cinnamon and nutmeg and also florals such as ylang ylang, rose, jasmine and geranium. Lavabre (1990) also comments that fir and pine can improve blends containing oils of the Myrtaceae and the order Coniferae.

Section 2

The Essential Oils of Aromatherapy

SECTION 2.1
THE ANGIOSPERMAE

Plants are classified in two large groups, known as the Angiospermae and the Gymnospermae. Both these groups, known as 'classes' of the plant kingdom, contain aromatic plants whose volatile oils are used in aromatherapy. The Angiosperms are the flowering plants and the Gymnosperms are the conifers. The Angiospermae is the most successful and diverse group of organisms on the earth.

CLASSIFICATION

The class Angiospermae is divided into two subclasses, based on the structure of the food storage organs (cotyledons) in their seeds: the monocotyledons and the dicotyledons. Other significant differences are the patterns of veins in the leaves, the distribution of vascular bundles in the stems, and flower structure. Monocots have veins that lie parallel to each other, while in dicots a network pattern is apparent. In monocot stems, the vascular bundles are randomly scattered, and in dicots they form a radial pattern. The flower structure of monocots is based on petals in threes, or multiples thereof, and in dicots four, five or multiples.

In the subclass of Monocotyledons, significant families (for essential oils) include the Agavaceae, Amaryllidaceae, Liliaceae, Orchidaceae, Poaceae and Zingiberaceae.

The subclass of Dicotyledons has a larger number of families of significance to essential oil studies, notably the Annonaceae,

Apiaceae, Asteraceae, Burseraceae, Caryophyllaceae, Geraniaceae, Illiciaceae, Lamiaceae, Lauraceae, Mimosaceae, Myristicaceae, Myrtaceae, Oleaceae, Piperaceae, Rosaceae, Rutaceae, Santalaceae, Styraceae, Tiliaceae and Violaceae.

This section contains an exploration of these families and their essential oils in alphabetical order according to their Latin names. (An index containing the common and botanical names can be found at the back of this book.)

Annonaceae Family

This family of tropical species belongs to the order Magnoliales. The Annonaceae has 120 genera, but only one genus is of significance from the essential oil perspective. Cananga was probably from south-east Asia, although now it has been naturalised in many other parts of the Pacific basin. It is particularly common in the Philippines. It has been introduced into many other parts of the world as an essential-oil-producing plant. The main oil-producing areas are now Indonesia and Madagascar.

Distillation was first carried out in the mid-nineteenth century, but essential oil production was halted during the First World War and now only small amounts of good quality oil are produced, mainly by smallholders.

Classification into two types (cananga and ylang ylang) was made in 1939 and both oils are now mainly produced in Java, although at one time Réunion was the acknowledged centre for the production of ylang ylang. At the beginning of the twentieth century, cananga was introduced to the Comoro Islands (Weiss 1997).

Genus *Cananga*

Cananga odorata var. *genuina* is the botanical source of ylang ylang oil. It is a tall tropical tree that produces numerous, yellow/green, highly scented flowers. Fractional steam distillation of the flowers produces four or five grades of essential oil; each fraction has a different chemical composition and odour. For more detail, see Weiss (1997). Sometimes suppliers may offer 'complete' oil but, according to Weiss (1997), this may well be cananga or adulterated third grade oil. An absolute is also produced, is intensely sweet and floral and is used in high-class perfumes and toiletries.

In aromatherapy, it is the fraction known as 'extra' that is most commonly used. However, this is not to say that the other fractions do not have therapeutic applications – they simply have not been investigated.

Ylang ylang extra is a pale yellow mobile liquid, with a sweet, persistent, floral odour that has a 'creamy' top note. Its chemical composition is very variable, however it will contain linalool (19%), terpenoid and aromatic esters including geranyl acetate, benzyl acetate and methyl salicylate (gives a slightly medicinal note), that collectively will account for up to 64%, phenyl methyl ethers (15%), sesquiterpenes such as farnesene and caryophyllene, and phenols including eugenol.

The extra has higher levels of *p*-cresyl methyl ether, methyl benzoate, linalool, methyl acetate and geranyl acetate than the other grades (Weiss 1997). Some major components of the various oils are shown in Table 2 (opposite).

Ylang ylang is credited with 'balancing', sedative and calming properties – possibly due to the ester and linalool content (Bowles 2003) – and is widely used to combat stress, tension, anxiety, tachycardia and insomnia (Price and Price 2007). It has antispasmodic properties and may help with cramp and colic (Price and Price 2007), and muscular tension. It can also be of use in skincare – especially helping with oily skin/acne. Kerr (1997) has produced a useful essential oil profile.

Table 2
Comparison of major components – ylang ylang and cananga oils

Component	Extra	1	2	3	Cananga
Linalool	10.3	5.5	3.2	2.0	1.7
Benzyl acetate	12.6	4.2	1.2	0.5	Neg.
β-caryophyllene	6.8	11.5	12.8	16.3	37.0
Farnesene	18.0	16.8	17.0	21.0	12.2
δ-cardinene	8.9	15.1	20.4	16.3	5.4
Benzyl benzoate	4.3	8.5	9.7	5.3	2.9
α-caryophyllene	3.1	4.2	4.1	8.8	10.5

From Weiss (1997)

Table 3
Ylang ylang essential oil in aromatherapy

System	Ylang ylang with
Nervous (anxiety, stress, tension, frustration, insomnia)	Frankincense, lavender, sandalwood, bergamot
Musculoskeletal and digestive (cramp)	Juniper berry, grapefruit, black pepper, ginger, clove bud, cinnamon leaf
Integumentary	Sandalwood, palmarosa, bergamot

Cananga odorata var. *macrophylla* produces cananga oil. The cananga tree is a fast-growing, medium to tall evergreen tree. The wood is not valuable. Leaves are many, thin, alternate and oblong and the numerous clusters of flowers are large, yellow-green and heavily scented. They consist of three sepals and six lanceolate petals about 4–8cm in length. Flowers are often borne throughout the year (Weiss 1997).

The oil is steam distilled and contains largely alcohols, at more than 30%, and esters at about 15% (Price and Price 2007), although there is wide variation and monoterpenes, phenols, sesquiterpenes, aldehydes and ketones are also present. The oil is pale yellow to pale orange and mobile with a sweet floral and powerful odour. According to Lawless (1996) the oil is a greenish-yellow viscous liquid with a sweet, floral and heavy scent. Here, it is classed as a base note.

C. latifolia also produces an essential oil, however, this has no commercial importance.

Apiaceae Family

This family, also known as the Umbelliferae, has many essential-oil-producing species that are of significance to aromatherapy practice. The members of this family are mainly found in temperate regions, or mountainous areas of the tropics. They may be herbs, shrubs or trees; however, they all produce flowers where all the petioles arise from the top of the stem – this form is known as an *umbel* (umbrella-like). Many of the essential oils obtained from this family have characteristically sweet, often anisic odours, partly due to the presence of constituents known as phenolic ethers.

It is impossible to assign general therapeutic actions to such a diverse group, but it is worth noting that many essential oils from the Apiaceae are derived from spices, flavourings, etc. that are reputed to be digestive aids, e.g. dill, caraway, parsley, aniseed. Many of these oils, e.g. sweet fennel and lovage, are also said to have diuretic and depurative properties.

As the essential oils come from a wide range of genera, the individual species of importance are listed below.

Anethum graveolens – dill. Dill essential oil is obtained from the fruit or seeds of the herb. It has a light, fresh, spicy, caraway-like odour. Dill seed oil contains 30–60% *d*-carvone. According to Lawless (1992, 1995), its main uses in aromatherapy are to support the digestive system (colic, dyspepsia, flatulence and indigestion).

Angelica archangelica – angelica. Angelica essential oil is obtained from the rhizome/root of this large, hairy aromatic plant. The essential oil has a rich, herbaceous, earthy odour

(Lawless 1992, 1995). The main chemical constituents are α-pinene (25%), 1,8-cineole (14.5%) and β-phellandrene (13.5%) (Bowles 2003). However, angelica root oil is phototoxic due to the presence of bergapten.

It is indicated for the respiratory system, circulation, muscles and joints, especially toxic accumulations, for the digestive system, anorexia, and for fatigue and stress/tension (Lawless 1992). The presence of α-pinene and 1,8-cineole would certainly support its reputed antispasmodic and expectorant properties and indications for the respiratory system.

Anthriscus cerefolium – chervil. Chervil essential oil is distilled from the seeds, fruit or leaves of this annual herb. The essential oil has a sweet, anisic (aniseed-like) odour and is dominated by estragole (methyl chavicol). For this reason, Lawless (1992) and Tisserand and Balacs (1995) suggest that it does not have a place in aromatherapy. It is not commercially available.

Carum carvi – caraway. Caraway essential oil is obtained from the seed/fruit of the large biennial herb. Often the essential oil is rectified to improve the odour. The rectified oil has a strong, warm, sweet, spicy odour that is closely related to the smell of the dried seed. The dominant constituent is *d*-carvone – present at 50%. It also contains 46% limonene and small amounts of cis-dihydrocarvone, myrcene and others (Bowles 2003).

According to Lawless, its main uses in aromatherapy are for the respiratory system – the dominant ketone may bestow mucolytic properties (Bowles 2003) – and the digestive system, the indications being very similar to those for dill and angelica essential oils.

Coriandrum sativum – coriander. Coriander essential oil is distilled from the seeds of the tall annual herb. It is a colourless/pale yellow mobile liquid that has a sweet, spicy, woody odour. Most coriander oil is produced in Europe (Croatia) (Lawless 1995).

The chemical composition varies according to the source and the ripeness of seeds. Price and Price (1999) report that the linalool content varies from 60 to 87%, making this the very dominant constituent, followed by monoterpenes at between 10 and 20%.

Table 4
Coriander seed essential oil in aromatherapy

System	Coriander seed with
Digestive	Dill, caraway, cardamom, nutmeg, sweet fennel, lavender, black pepper, citrus oils
Musculoskeletal (arthritis, rheumatism)	Nutmeg, sweet fennel, grapefruit, black pepper, lavender
Nervous (tension, stress, anxiety, depression, fatigue, lethargy, debility, convalescence)	Lavender, citrus oils, palmarosa, geranium, rosewood, rose, jasmine

Price and Price (1999) also highlight several therapeutic actions. Antibacterial/anti-infectious actions indicate that coriander seed oil is useful for respiratory and urinary tract infections, while antispasmodic, stomachic and carminative properties make it an important oil for the digestive system.

Like angelica, it is indicated for anorexia. It is also indicated as an analgesic for osteoarthritic and rheumatic pain. Price and Price (1999) also state that it has euphoric actions. The high linalool content may indeed confer the anti-infectious, antispasmodic, analgesic and sedative properties (Bowles 2003) of this versatile essential oil.

Cuminum cyminum – cumin. Cumin essential oil is obtained from the ripe seeds of this annual herb (it is closely related to coriander). However, the essential oil is very different, being dominated by cuminaldehyde at 20–40% (Tisserand and Balacs 1995). It can be used to support the digestive system and nervous system and aid with 'toxic accumulations' (Lawless 1992). Cumin essential oil is not widely used in aromatherapy – mainly as it is strongly phototoxic, and possibly because of its distinctive aroma, reminiscent of curry.

Ferula galbaniflua – galbanum. Galbanum essential oil is obtained by distillation of the oleoresin that exudes from this large perennial herb. The oleoresin is from the Middle East, but most of the essential oil is distilled in Europe.

The essential oil is a colourless/pale yellow mobile liquid with a powerful, fresh green odour, reminiscent of green bell peppers. This distinctive green note is due to the presence of trace amounts of a nitrogen-containing pyrazine, 2-methoxy-3-I-butylpyrazine (Gimelli 2001). Galbanum essential oil is dominated by monoterpenes including the pinenes and limonene. Its main uses in aromatherapy, according to Lawless (1992) are for the skin (cicatrisant, anti-inflammatory and antiseptic qualities), the musculoskeletal system (analgesic, circulatory stimulant) and the respiratory system (expectorant and antispasmodic), and as a general tonic. This essential oil is not included in the majority of aromatherapy texts; therefore it is underused in current Anglo-Saxon aromatherapy practice.

Table 5
Galbanum essential oil in aromatherapy

System	Galbanum with
Integumentary (indicated for mature skin)	Lavender, geranium, sandalwood, patchouli, jasmine/violet leaf
Musculoskeletal (aches and pains)	Lavender, black pepper, Roman and German chamomile, clary sage
Nervous (tension, stress, fatigue, lethargy)	Lavender, geranium, rosewood, hyacinth, violet leaf
Respiratory	Scots pine, fir, rosemary, Atlas cedarwood, lemon

Foeniculum vulgare var. *dulce* – sweet fennel. Sweet fennel essential oil is obtained from the seeds of this biennial herb. The main countries of origin are France, Italy, Spain, Turkey and Bulgaria. The essential oil is a pale yellow mobile liquid with a characteristic fresh, sweet, anise and earthy aroma.

The proportions of its main chemical constituents are somewhat variable and dependent on the source material (Lawless 1992). According to Bowles (2003), they are typically trans-anethole at 80%, limonene at 6% and estragole at 4.5%.

A ketone, fenchone, may also be present as a minor constituent; this is dominant in the essential oil obtained from the bitter fennel, *F. vulgare* var. *amara*.

It has been suggested that sweet fennel oil may also have mild oestrogenic qualities, possibly conferred by the presence of trans-anethole (Price and Price 1999). This compound is a phenolic ether that, in large doses, can produce psychotropic effects; but this is highly unlikely in Anglo-Saxon aromatherapy practice. Trans-anethole has also been shown to exert analgesic and antispasmodic effects (Tisserand and Balacs 1995).

Sweet fennel oil has been ascribed a wide range of therapeutic actions, and is cited in most texts as being of great value in several areas of aromatherapy practice, e.g. the respiratory, digestive and female reproductive systems.

According to Price and Price (1999), sweet fennel oil is particularly useful for its therapeutic actions on the digestive system (antispasmodic, carminative). It is also indicated for Pre-Menstral Syndrome (PMS) and menopause symptoms, not simply because of its oestrogenic qualities but also its other properties, which may alleviate associated symptoms such as oedema (diuretic), bloating (carminative) and breast engorgement (decongestant). Cellulite is also mentioned.

It is cited as a respiratory tonic, but its bronchodilatory action is not emphasised. Similarly, the analgesic quality is not highlighted.

This is an extremely versatile and useful oil in aromatherapy but should always be used in low doses. Most authors suggest caution in the following situations: pregnancy, oestrogen-dependent cancers and compromised liver function.

Table 6
Sweet fennel essential oil in aromatherapy

System	Sweet fennel with
Female reproductive	Geranium, juniper berry, clary sage, sage
Digestive	Sweet marjoram, black pepper, sweet orange, mandarin, clary sage, peppermint
Respiratory	*Eucalyptus* spp. (1,8-cineole types), lemon

Levisticum officinale – lovage. An essential oil can be distilled from both the roots and the aerial parts of this large, aromatic, perennial herb. The oil from the roots is reminiscent of celery. Little information is available, as it is not used much in aromatherapy practice. The essential oil is composed mainly of phthalides (70%) (Lawless 1992) – these include butylidene and its derivatives and ligostilides; coumarins and furocoumarins are also present (Lawless 1995). Lawless suggests that it may have uses for the accumulation of toxins, the digestive system and the genito-urinary system.

Petroselinum sativum – parsley. Parsley seed oil is not often used in aromatherapy, mainly due to the presence of apiol, a phenolic ether that can (if abused) cause many serious problems, e.g. coma, respiratory depression, hypotension and kidney damage. There are three chemotypes, however, a 'typical' parsley seed essential oil will contain myristicin (a phenolic ether) at around 28%, TMAB (2,3,4,5-tetramethoxyallylbenzene) at 23% and parsley apiol at 21% (Tisserand and Balacs 1995). Parsley seed oil should only be used with caution externally; it is contraindicated in pregnancy and it should not be taken orally.

Pimpinella anisum – aniseed, anise. This is misnamed, as it is actually the fruit that is used. The essential oil has a warm, spicy, sweet odour, characteristic of the herb. It has a very high proportion of trans-anethole – up to 90%. Although this has therapeutic actions (see sweet fennel) the very high level here means that aniseed should be used with caution, avoiding it in breast-feeding, liver disease, oestrogen-dependent cancers, alcoholism, pregnancy, endometriosis, and paracetamol use (Tisserand and Balacs 1995).

Asteraceae Family

This family is also called the Compositae, and is often referred to as the 'daisy' family. Essential oils obtained from this family are quite diverse, however many contain fairly large quantities of a group of chemicals known as sesquiterpenoid lactones. Lactones are frequently implicated in allergic skin reactions. Bowles (2003) comments that plants from this family, e.g. chrysanthemums, are often responsible for allergic contact dermatitis in the floristry profession. However, members of this family produce several important essential oils..

Achillea millefolium – yarrow. Yarrow is a large perennial herb with finely dissected leaves and numerous flower heads. The essential oil is obtained from the dried flowering herb, and is a dark blue or greenish olive mobile liquid (Lawless 1992). There are several chemotypes (Tisserand and Balacs 1995), the camphor and chamazulene being the most commonly available. Its odour is herbaceous with a camphoraceous note, but this depends on the chemical composition.

According to Tisserand and Balacs (1995), notable constituents are camphor (a neurotoxic ketone) at 10–20%, 1,8-cineole at 14% and borneol at 9%. However, Lawless states that the dominant constituent is 'azulene' at up to 51%. This is presumably chamazulene, the inky blue sesquiterpene with powerful anti-inflammatory properties (see also German chamomile). The sabinene, 1,8-cineole and chamazulene chemotypes do not present a hazard, but the camphor chemotype should be used with caution and is contraindicated via the oral route in pregnancy, epilepsy and fever (Tisserand and Balacs 1995).

Therapeutically, yarrow essential oil is noted for its anticatarrhal/decongestant, anti-inflammatory, vasodilatory and cicatrisant qualities (Price and Price 2007) and, according to Tisserand and Balacs (1995), is a substitute for German chamomile, see also Whitton (1994).

Table 7
Yarrow essential oil in aromatherapy

System	Yarrow with
Musculoskeletal (pain/inflammation)	Lavender, Scots pine, sweet marjoram, grapefruit, black pepper, juniper berry
Cardiovascular (varicose veins and ulcers)	Lavender, cypress, patchouli, lemon, geranium

Artemisia vulgaris and *Artemisia arborescens* – mugwort and great mugwort. Mugwort essential oils are obtained from the leaves and flowering tops of these large perennial herbs. Like *A. absinthium*, the mugworts have a tradition of medicinal use, but contain large amounts of thujone, rendering the essential oils toxic and neurotoxic (Lawless 1992). There are many other species of *Artemisia* that yield essential oils – all containing high levels of thujone and some containing 'artemisia ketone'. Most are deemed unsuitable for aromatherapeutic use.

Artemisia absinthium – wormwood. Absinthium oil is obtained from the leaves and flowering tops of the large perennial. Although the herb has a long tradition of medicinal use, the essential oil is severely toxic and neurotoxic and is not used in aromatherapy (Tisserand and Balacs 1995). It contains high levels of thujone (34–71%).

Artemisia draconculis – tarragon. Tarragon oil is obtained from the leaves of this perennial that is widely used in cooking. The essential oil is dominated by estragole. This phenolic ether is present in such large amounts in tarragon oil that it is deemed unsuitable for use in aromatherapy (Tisserand and Balacs 1995). For more information about estragole, see the profile of basil essential oil.

Anthemis nobilis (also called *Chaemamelum nobile*) – Roman chamomile. The essential oil is obtained from the daisy-like flowers of this creeping perennial. It has a distinctive pale blue colour and a strong, fruity (apple), herbaceous odour. The main geographical sources are Hungary, France and Italy (Lawless 1992). According to Bowles (2003), a typical essential oil

(Japanese) contains isobutyl angelate at 35.9%, 2-methyl butyl angelate at 15.3% and methallyl angelate at 8.7%. Roman chamomile essential oil is dominated by such non-terpenoid esters derived from short chain parent alcohols. Bowles (2000, 2003) cites Franchomme and Pénoël (1990), who state that such esters are oriented towards the head and the psyche, with cephalic and psychotropic characteristics. Additionally, isobutyl angelate is hailed as 'one of the grand antispasmodics of the pharmacopoeia'. In Anglo-Saxon aromatherapy, Roman chamomile is widely used as an antispasmodic, sedative and anti-inflammatory (Price and Price 2007). For a profile of the chamomiles, see Kerr (1998).

Table 8
Roman chamomile essential oil in aromatherapy

System	Roman chamomile with
Musculoskeletal (tension/pain/inflammation)	Lavender, ginger, plai, sweet marjoram, bergamot, lemongrass
Nervous (insomnia*, stress, tension, headache/migraine**)	Lavender*, neroli*, clary sage, geranium, jasmine, citrus oils, peppermint**
Integumentary (eczema, inflammation, wound healing)	Lavender, *Helichrysum angustifolium*, bergamot, geranium, vetivert, patchouli, sandalwood, yarrow, rose

The asterisks indicate a particular relationship between the condition and the oil (and are marked by a single or double asterisk)

Helichrysum angustifolium (H. italicum) and *H. orientale* (essential oil), *H. stoechas* (absolute) – immortelle, everlasting. The essential oil from *Helichrysum angustifolium (H. italicum)* is the one used in aromatherapy practice. It is obtained from the flowering tops of this large aromatic herb, and is a pale yellow mobile liquid with a powerful, rich, sweet, honey-like odour. Chemically, it is dominated by α-pinene (21.7%), γ-curcumene (10.4%) and italidiones (diketones) at 8%. Italidiones (especially those found in *H. italicum* ssp. *serotinum*) are reputed to have antihaematomal properties (Bowles 2003) and thus are often used for bruises and trauma to the superficial soft tissues. Pénoël (1991), as cited by Price and Price (2007), states that helichrysum is sometimes called the super arnica of aromatherapy. (Homoeopathic arnica is renowned for the healing of trauma.)

Table 9
***Helichrysum* essential oil in aromatherapy**

System	*Helichrysum* with
Musculoskeletal (arthritic conditions)	Wintergreen or sweet birch (Price and Price 2007)
Integumentary (eczema, wound healing, inflammation)	Lavender, Roman chamomile, geranium, yarrow, vetivert, patchouli, sandalwood, cypress, rose
Trauma	Neat or diluted at 10–50% (Price and Price 2007)
Immune (allergic responses)	Rose, sandalwood, German chamomile

It would seem that *Helichrysum* does have some unusual therapeutic properties. Price and Price (2007) suggest that it is anti-allergenic – so could be of help in cases of asthma, hay fever or eczema. Its cicatrisant properties suggest that it can be used to aid skin regeneration and help with wound healing. Finally, it is a useful phlebotonic – Price and Price (2007) claim that it is indicated for couperose skin (red veins), haematoma (even old), thrombosis and prevention of bruises.

Inula graveolens and *I. helenium* – sweet inula and elecampane. Both essential oils are obtained from the dried roots and rhizomes of the perennial daisy-like plants, and both are characterised by the presence of chemicals known as lactones. Elecampane essential oil is not used in aromatherapy because of the high risk of causing severe sensitisation (Lawless 1992, Tisserand and Balacs 1995) due to the large amounts of a sesquiterpenoid lactone known as alantolactone (52%) and *iso*-alantolactone (33%).

Sweet inula is a deep green essential oil (Lawless 1992) without the sensitisation capacity of elecampane. Schnaubelt (1995) writes that it contains 50% bornyl acetate with traces of the sesquiterpene lactones; Tisserand and Balacs (1995) maintain it contains mainly bornyl acetate and camphene.

Inula is mainly used in French aromatherapy, probably due to the influence of Franchomme, cited in Lawless (1992) and Schnaubelt (1995), who states that it is the strongest mucolytic found in aromatherapy. This effect occurs even below the odour threshold. Schnaubelt (1995) recommends that it is administered by diffusion, and is invaluable for all bronchitis and catarrhal conditions of the throat/nose and also spasmodic conditions affecting the respiratory tract.

Matricaria recutita – German chamomile. The essential oil is obtained from the daisy-like flowers of an annual herb (Lawless 1992). It is a deep inky blue liquid – the colour is due to a constituent called chamazulene, formed during the distillation process from the parent chemical, matricine, which is found in the flowers.

German chamomile oil is characterised by the presence of chamazulene, farnesene (both sesquiterpenes) and α–bisabolol (a sesquiterpene alcohol). There are several chemotypes, so there is a wide variation in the proportions of these. Price and Price (2007) indicate that chamazulene ranges from 1% to 35%; Bowles (2003) gives a chamazulene content of 17%. The α–bisabolol content ranges from 2–67% (Price and Price 2007), while the farnesene content (*trans*-α–farnesene) is in the region of 27%. Bisabolol oxides (A and B) are also significant – Price and Price (2007) state that the dominant α–bisabolol oxide content can range from 0 to 55%. This is a case where many of the therapeutic properties ascribed to an essential oil can be related to its chemical constituents. Price and Price (2007) highlight its anti-inflammatory actions, and their observations include research that has been done investigating its anti-allergenic potential.

Chamazulene itself has interesting effects. Bowles (2003) states that it is anti-inflammatory in vivo, citing the work of Safayhi *et al* (1994) who suggest that the mechanism of this effect is the blocking of the formation of leukotriene B4, an inflammatory mediator produced by neutrophils at sites of inflammation. Mills (1991), cited in Price and Price (2007), also states that chamazulene (and bisabolol) are not only anti-inflammatory but also antispasmodic, and can reduce histamine-induced reactions. This would suggest that German chamomile oil has applications in cases of allergic problems including hay fever and some types of asthma and eczema. When referring to 'azulenes' Mills (1991), cited in Price and Price (2007), suggests that they can 'calm the nervous system both peripherally as in nervous tension and centrally as in anxiety, nervous tension and headaches...'

The other significant component in German chamomile is α–bisabolol. This is a sesquiterpene alcohol with enormous therapeutic potential. It is non toxic and non irritant, more anti-inflammatory than chamazulene (Bowles 2003) and research has also indicated that α–bisabolol has 'a strikingly efficient and potent cytotoxic effect on human and rat malignant glioma cell lines' (Cavalieri *et al* 2004), leading to the conclusion that α–bisabolol may have use in clinical treatment of glioma (a highly malignant brain tumour).

Table 10
German chamomile essential oil in aromatherapy

System	German chamomile with
Musculoskeletal (inflammation, spasm)	Lavender and others appropriate to circumstances
Integumentary (inflammation, eczema, allergy, irritation, wounds)	Lavender, *Helichrysum*, vetivert, patchouli, rose
Immune (hay fever)	Peppermint, sandalwood, rose, lavender

Ormenis multicaulis – Moroccan chamomile. The essential oil is distilled from the flowers of this species (aka *O. mixta*) that is common in the Mediterranean region. It belongs to the same botanical family as the German and Roman chamomiles, but its essential oil is very different and should not be considered as a 'substitute' (Lawless 1992). It does not have a tradition of use in aromatherapy practice.

Tisserand and Balacs (1995) state that its major components are α-pinene and artemisia alcohol, neither of which is particularly hazardous.

Tagetes minuta, T. glandulifera – tagetes or 'Mexican marigold'. Tagetes essential oil is distilled from the flowering tops of this annual herb. It has a distinctive green, fruity, herbal odour, which is used in perfumery to impart apple notes (Williams 2000).

The main constituent of this essential oil is a ketone – tagetone – present at 50–60%; however, the presence of a group of chemicals known as furanocoumarins means that tagetes oil is strongly phototoxic. For this reason, it is not widely used in aromatherapy. Perhaps this is compounded by Lawless's (1992) reference to Arctander (1960) – 'it is quite possible that "tagetone" (the main constituent) is harmful to the human organism.'

Burseraceae Family

This family includes some of the shrubs and trees that exude fragrant oleogum resins that can be extracted to produce essential oils and absolutes. Many of these species, e.g. frankincense, oponopax and myrrh, have biblical or Middle Eastern connotations. Several essential oils from this family are used in aromatherapy practice, mainly to aid the respiratory system and the skin, although other uses are reported.

Boswellia carteri – frankincense. Also called olibanum, frankincense essential oil is obtained from an oleo-gum resin formed in specialised resin ducts in the tissues of the small tree that grows in north-east Africa. When incisions are made in the bark, the milky white resin exudes and solidifies in tear-shaped amber drops. These are harvested and usually exported to Europe for distillation of the essential oil (Lawless 1995).

The essential oil is a pale yellow mobile liquid that has a spicy, woody odour with lemony top notes and a balsamic dryout (Williams 2000). According to Bowles (2003), its dominant chemical constituent is α–pinene at 34.5%, followed by α–phellandrene at 14.6% and para-cymene at 14%. These are all classed as monoterpenes, a large group of chemicals often attributed with stimulating, decongestant and analgesic qualities.

Price and Price (2007) highlight frankincense essential oil's anticatarrhal, antidepressant and immunostimulant properties, therefore this oil is particularly useful for the respiratory congestion associated with asthma and bronchitis, for those with compromised immune systems and for alleviating anxiety and depression.

Table 11
Frankincense essential oil in aromatherapy

System	Frankincense with
Respiratory (catarrh, asthma, bronchitis)	Pine, lemon, bergamot, ginger, lavender. Also with sandalwood, Atlas cedarwood
Nervous (anxiety, stress, tension, depression)	Lavender, neroli, geranium, jasmine, lime, mandarin, sandalwood
Immune (colds, 'flu, ME, convalescence)	Lavender, rosewood, palmarosa

Canarium luzonicum – elemi. Elemi essential oil is distilled from a gum-like pathological exudate from this large tropical tree. Although the gum has a long tradition of use, including its application as an embalming agent in ancient Egypt (Lawless 1992), it is not used or used only with great caution in aromatherapy, as the essential oil may be carcinogenic (Tisserand and Balacs 1995).

This is due to the presence of a chemical known as elemicin, present at between 3 and 12%. However, the dominant constituent of elemi essential oil is the monoterpene *d*-limonene. This could quench the potential for carcinogenesis, as *d*-limonene could well have cancer-prevention properties (Tisserand and Balacs 1995, Bowles 2003), leading Tisserand and Balacs to state that 'the chances of elemi oil causing serious problems in aromatherapy seem remote'.

Commiphora erythraea – opopanax. Like elemi, opopanax essential oil is obtained from a gum, but the oil is phototoxic and is not produced in significant quantities. Information on opopanax is limited – therefore it is not widely used in contemporary aromatherapy practice.

Commiphora myrrha – myrrh. Myrrh essential oil is distilled from crude myrrh oleoresin. The *Commiphora* genus is compromised of small trees and shrubs native to the Red Sea region. They have specialised resin ducts that exude an oleoresin – see frankincense (above) – and the harvesting and processing is similar. Myrrh essential oil is a pale yellow mobile liquid with a sweet, spicy medicinal odour.

A detailed breakdown of this chemically complex oil may be found in Price and Price (2007). Suffice it to say that it is dominated by sesquiterpenols – a group of constituents associated with some very interesting therapeutic actions, including anti-inflammatory effects, and a ketone known as curzerenone.

Myrrh essential oil does indeed have an anti-inflammatory effect (Bowles 2003). Price and Price (2007), however, emphasise its antiseptic qualities, its indications for the urinary tract and for cleansing sores and ulcers. They do cite Bartram (1995), who wrote that myrrh was a leucocytogenic agent, which is bacteriostatic against *Staphy-lococcus aureus* and other Gram-positive bacteria, and also commented that it is perhaps the most widely used herbal antiseptic.

Lawless (1992 and 1995) and Price and Price (2007) concur that myrrh is also indicated for healing the skin (cicatrisant) and for the respiratory system (expectorant).

Table 12
Myrrh essential oil in aromatherapy

System	Myrrh with
Respiratory (congestion, bronchitis laryngitis)	Frankincense, thyme, sandalwood
Integumentary (skin and wound healing)	Lavender, patchouli, geranium
Genito-urinary (urinary tract infections, cystitis, pruritis, thrush)	Lavender, juniper berry, bergamot, sandalwood

Geraniaceae Family

There are five genera in the Geraniaceae. Of these, only the genus *Pelargonium* (stork's bill) and the genus *Geranium* (crane's bill) are essential-oil producers. The term geranium is commonly used to refer to both pelargonium and geranium, and it is in fact the *Pelargonium* species that are cultivated to produce 'geranium' essential oil. The only species of the genus *Geranium* that is grown for essential oil production is *Geranium macrorrhizum*, the essential oil being known as zdravetz oil. For an exploration of this unusual essential oil, see Brud and Ogyanov (1995). They expand on the chemistry, exploring the cyclic ketone germacrone and suggest that it should be a useful antimicrobical and have potential antitumoural properties.

Zdravetz oil has a persistent odour similar to clary sage. It is used in perfumery and has historical use as an aphrodisiac; chemically it is dominated by germacrol (Jouhar 1991).

A close study of geranium oils will highlight the intricacies of taxonomy, and also the influences of ecological factors, such as geography and growth conditions, on essential oil quality and odour.

Genus *Pelargonium*

Geranium essential oil is one of the most widely used oils in aromatherapy practice. The Pelargonium genus was first named in South Africa. *P. graveolens* was introduced to Britain in the 1700s and was cultivated for essential oil for the first time in the early nineteenth century around Grasse in France. The main area of cultivation then moved to Réunion (*P. capitatum x P. radens*), and now includes Algeria, Morocco and Egypt (Weiss 1997), but also India (plants from Réunion) and China (*P. roseum*). The genus contains about 250 species (Van der Walt 1977 and 1985) and the four species particularly used in essential-oil production are *P. graveolens*, *P. odoratissimum*, *P. capitatum* and *P. radens*, but there is also *P. roseum*, a hybrid of *P. graveolens*.

P. graveolens is a many-branched, small, perennial shrub. The leaves are fragrant with a minty scent and the plant bears pink, rosy or pale purple flowers in small umbels of 3–7 flowers.

P. odoratissimum has a more creeping or trailing habit, with apple-scented leaves and bears umbels of 3–10 tiny white or pink flowers with red spots.

P. radens is more erect with mint-scented leaves and umbels of 3–8 pale purple flowers.

P. capitatum is another creeping species, this time with rose-scented leaves and tiny sessile flowers. The oil yield from this species is very low and also very variable in composition.

P. capitatum x P. radens, which became known as the 'Bourbon' type or Rose geranium, is an erect and compact shrub with rose-scented leaves and umbels of 3–10 small, rose-violet-coloured flowers.

The oil is found in glands throughout the green parts of the plant. Geranium oil is steam or hydro-distilled from the fresh herbage. The oil is usually designated by country of origin. Much adulteration occurs, but oils from Egypt and Réunion are usually good quality (Weiss 1997). Oil from Réunion is olive green with a brownish tinge and has a rosy, sweet and fruity aroma; that from Morocco is dark to mid yellow with a sweet, rosy and herbaceous aroma; Egyptian oil is yellowish green with a similar aroma to that from Morocco; and Chinese oil is a dark olive green with a harsher odour than Réunion, but at the same time more lemony and rosy, sweet and herbaceous (Weiss 1997).

The major constituents include the alcohols citronellol, geraniol and linalool (55–65%), esters (15%) and ketones such as iso-menthone (1–8%) (Price and Price 2007) and, because of the variability, the proportions of each of these affect the aroma (Weiss 1997). Aldehydes (neral, geranial, and citronellal) up to 10% are found in the Bourbon variety (Price and Price 2007). Price and Price (2007) also state that oxides are found only in the Chinese variety. A comparison is shown in Table 13. For a review of the botany and chemistry of geranium oil, see Lis-Balchin (1996).

Geranium oil is used as an insecticide, nematicide and antifungal (Weiss 1997). Lawless (1996) suggests it might be used for skincare (acne and oily skin), oedema, poor circulation and cellulitis, sore throats, premenstrual syndrome and menopause, to stimulate the adrenocortical glands, as well as for nervous tension and stress. It is fungicidal, probably due to geraniol and aldehydes, contains anti-inflammatory esters and seems to be more 'balancing' than sedative. Some might suggest that it is a balancer of mood swings related to hormones (Bowles 2003), possibly by acting on the adrenocortical glands. Geranium has certainly been shown to reduce anxiety in inhalation (Morris *et al* 1995).

Table 13
Comparison of the main chemical constituents of geranium oil

Component	Algeria	China	Egypt	Morocco	Réunion
Iso-menthone	5.38	5.70	5.39	5.20	7.20
Linalool	5.26	3.96	9.47	6.80	12.90
Citronellyl formate	0.57	11.35	6.74	6.02	8.37
Geranyl formate	5.90	1.92	4.75	6.55	7.55
Citronellol	22.90	40.23	27.40	19.28	21.28
Geraniol	17.07	6.45	18.00	18.40	17.45
10-Epi-gamma eudesmol	4.20	–	4.00	5.10	–

From Weiss (1997)

Table 14
Geranium essential oil in aromatherapy

System	Geranium with
Integumentary	Lavender, bergamot, palmarosa, sandalwood, tea tree
Female reproductive	Sweet fennel, clary sage, rose, cypress
Nervous (anxiety, mood swings, post-natal depression)	Lavender, bergamot, clary sage, lemon, grapefruit, mandarin

Illiciaceae Family

In this family (also referred to as the Magnoliaceae), the genus *Illicium* comprises around forty species of trees and shrubs. However, only one species, *Illicium verum*, is of importance in aromatherapy. Its essential oil should not be confused with aniseed (*Pimpinella anisum*), which it resembles.

Illicium verum – star anise, Chinese star anise. Star anise yields an essential oil from the fully ripe, star-shaped fruits of the tall evergreen. The essential oil is a colourless or pale yellow liquid with a sweet, anise, liquorice-like odour (Lawless 1995). Star anise contains around 70% trans-anethole (Bowles 2003), the phenolic ether also found in sweet fennel essential oil, and often ascribed 'oestrogenic' properties Weiss (2002). Trans-anethole may also have antispasmodic and anaesthetic effects (Bowles 2003), hence its use in aromatherapy for muscular aches and pains, colic and cramp. Star anise is also used for the respiratory system because of its expectorant properties (Lawless 1995). For reservations and cautions, see sweet fennel.

Table 15
Star anise essential oil in aromatherapy

System	Star anise with
Female reproductive	Rose, geranium, juniper berry
Digestive	Black pepper, coriander seed, cardamom, sweet orange, mandarin
Respiratory	Lemon, Scots pine

Lamiaceae Family

Older texts refer to this family as the Labiatae, where many essential oil-bearing plants are found. It is one of the ten largest families, comprising 3,200 species, which are mainly herbs or shrubs. Weiss (1997) comments that this family has a large number of species that produce essential oils and/or spices. Members of this family are distinguished by their flowers, which have discreet, gaping lips (hence the term *labiates*), opposite leaves and angular petioles, and a four-part ovary. In many cases the leaves are highly aromatic.

Typically, the volatile oil is found in glandular cells or glandular hairs located on the leaves. The genera and species of most importance in aromatherapy are described below.

Hyssopus officinalis – hyssop. Hyssop essential oil is obtained from the leaves and flowering tops of the perennial, woody herb. The essential oil is produced in Hungary and France, and it is a colourless/pale yellow green mobile liquid (Lawless 1995) that has a strong, camphoraceous, warm, spicy odour (Williams 2000).

Hyssop essential oil is not widely used because of the numerous contraindications associated with it – epilepsy, fever, pregnancy, and children less than two years. It is moderately toxic, and neurotoxic (it can cause convulsions). The components that are responsible for this are ketones – pinocamphone and iso-pinocamphone.

The Lavenders

The lavenders are aromatic, evergreen, woody shrubs, with a long tradition of use in folk medicine. They originated in the Mediterranean region and are now cultivated in many countries for their essential oils (Lawless 1992). Lavender essential oils are obtained by steam distillation of the flowering tops.

The essential oils were originally produced for the perfumery industry, however, in recent years lavender essential oil has become one of the most well known and popular essential oils. It is probably the most useful and versatile of the therapeutic essential oils.

Lavandula angustifolia, *L. vera* and *L. officinalis* are the true lavenders; they hybridise easily, therefore many subspecies (ssp.), for example *delphinensis* and many cultivars, are in existence. Other species in this genus include *L. latifolia* (also known as *L. spica* and its subspecies *fragrans*), which yields spike lavender essential oil, and *L. stoechas*, which yields an essential oil known as French lavender. The hybrid *Lavandula x intermedia* is a cross between true lavender and spike lavender; it yields an essential oil called lavandin.

Lavandula angustifolia is the botanical source of true lavender. The essential oil is produced in several countries including France, Spain, Bulgaria, Tasmania and the UK (Norfolk, Suffolk, Kent). It is a pale yellow/colourless mobile liquid and the odour will vary according to the geographical source.

Table 16
True lavender essential oil in aromatherapy

System	True lavender with
Nervous (*pain, *migraine, **insomnia, ***anxiety)	*Peppermint, clove bud, marjoram, **Roman Chamomile, neroli, ***geranium, ylang ylang, clary sage, frankincense, sandalwood, rose, bergamot and citrus oils
Musculoskeletal (aches and pains, tension)	Marjoram, rosemary, clary sage, juniper berry, basil, lemon, lemongrass, black pepper, ginger, plai
Integumentary (*irritation, *eczema, **infection, ***itching, ****healing, *****phlebitis)	*Geranium, rose, sandalwood, patchouli, vetivert, **tea tree, ***tea tree, bergamot, peppermint, ****Helichrysum*, myrrh, *****patchouli, bergamot

The asterisks indicate a particular relationship between the condition and the oil (and will be marked by a corresponding number of asterisks)

Lavender has a herbal, fruity, floral, woody aroma, with a nondescript dryout (Williams 2000) – true lavender 40/42 is typical. The '40/42' refers to its linalyl acetate content. Linalyl acetate can be present at anywhere between 36% and 53% (Price and Price 2007). This component, along with linalool (present at between 26–49%), may contribute to lavender's sedative effect on mice (Buchbauer *et al* 1991 cited in Bowles 2003, p. 92) and in humans (Buchbauer *et al* 1993).

In addition to being calming and sedative, lavender has several other therapeutic properties. Price and Price (2007) note that lavender is also analgesic, anti-inflammatory, antispasmodic, and cicatrising.

L. latifolia (also known as *L. spica*) – spike lavender. Spike lavender essential oil is quite different from true lavender in odour, chemistry and, consequently, in its therapeutic applications. It has a camphoraceous, herbal, woody odour (Williams 2000) – it is sharper and fresher, lacking the softer, floral/fruity notes of true lavender. This is because it contains 1,8-cineole at 36.3%, linalool at 30.3% and camphor (the ketone) at 8% (Bowles 2003). 1,8-cineole is an oxide found in many essential oils – and in high amounts in many *Eucalyptus* oils. In large amounts, 1,8-cineole can have neurotropic effects (slurred speech, coma, convulsions), and it can cause respiratory irritation, as it is a rubefacient and mucous membrane irritant. However, 1,8-cineole is an expectorant, an anti-inflammatory in cases of bronchial asthma, and it may also be a stimulant of the trigeminal nerve – hence its ability to increase alertness (Bowles 2003). Buchbauer (1996) states that 1,8-cineole can increase cerebral blood flow, and has also suggested that it has spasmolytic properties (1993). Balacs

(1997), in a comprehensive review of cineole-rich oils, explores the pharmacokinetics of 1,8-cineole, emphasising that this compound is absorbed very quickly from the air into the bloodstream. The camphor (neurotoxic ketone) content is not high – true lavender has a camphor content of $<1\%$ (Tisserand and Balacs 1995) – but it is present in sufficient quantity to class it as an essential oil to be used with caution, and avoided in epilepsy, fever and pregnancy. Spike lavender is a stimulating essential oil, with mucolytic and expectorant properties. It can be useful for muscular aches and pains, and respiratory congestion. Its odour is very compatible with that of rosemary, *Eucalyptus* spp., pine, clove bud (and also true lavender and lavandin) – all of which would also be indicated for these complaints.

Lavandula stoechas – French lavender. French lavender essential oil (not to be confused with true lavender from France!) has a fairly high camphor content (15–30%) and a fenchone (another ketone) content of 45–50%, and so is best avoided in aromatherapy.

Lavandula x intermedia – lavandin. As you could expect from a cross between true and spike lavender, lavandin essential oil contains linalool (20–60%), linalyl acetate (15–50%), camphor (5–15%) and 1,8-cineole (5–25%). Again, this oil should be used with caution, due to the camphor content (Tisserand and Balacs 1995).

Melissa officinalis – melissa (lemon balm). Melissa essential oil is a pale yellow mobile liquid that has a citrus/herbal odour, which is little used (Williams 2000). This hesitation could be due to the fact that melissa essential oil is frequently adulterated, or even synthetic, and in the past it was difficult to purchase the genuine essential oil (Price and Price 2007). The yield is very low, and the oil commands a high price (Sorensen 2000).

Authentic, laboratory-distilled melissa contains around 80% of an aldehyde, citral (Sorensen 2000). Citral is the name given to a naturally occurring mixture of two aldehydes – geranial and neral – chemicals that are isomers (same molecular formula, minor differences in molecular structure). Yet another aldehyde, citronellal, is present and a high level of this is an indicator of adulteration (Sorensen 2000).

Many writers of aromatherapy books that are aimed at both the general public and the professional do ascribe therapeutic properties to melissa – notably that it is a calming, sedative essential oil (Price and Price 2007). Tisserand and Balacs (1995) suggest caution due to the citral content (it may cause sensitisation), while Price and Price (2007) suggest that care should be exercised if the oil is used on skin that is exposed to direct sunlight.

In fact, there is very little evidence to support melissa's therapeutic use (Sorensen 2000), other than speculation about the effects that citral may impart.

Mentha piperita hybrid – peppermint. Botanically, peppermint is a cross between *M. viridis* (spearmint) and *M. aquatica* (watermint). It is a widely cultivated perennial, whose essential oil is produced in many countries, including France and England (in Mitcham). Peppermint oil is extensively used in the flavour, fragrance and pharmaceutical industries.

It is a pale yellow or colourless mobile liquid, with a strong, fresh, minty, green odour (Williams 2000). This is mainly due to menthol (a monoterpene alcohol present at around 42%) and menthone (the corresponding ketone at 20%). Menthol produces a cooling sensation when applied to the skin and there is evidence to support its analgesic effects. Menthone is not a neurotoxic ketone although it may well have some of the properties attributed to ketones – notably their effects on mucosal secretions and wound-healing properties (Bowles 2003). These two constituents can at least partly account for the therapeutic properties associated with peppermint essential oil.

Price and Price (2007) give a long list of properties and indications, citing several research papers. In summary, the main uses for peppermint essential oil are for the respiratory system, especially bronchitis and asthma, as it is antispasmodic, expectorant and mucolytic; for the integumentary system, especially eczema, rashes and itching as it is anti-inflammatory, antipruritic and analgesic; for the nervous system/pain (migraine, neuralgia and sciatica) as it is analgesic and cephalic; and for the digestive system, especially indigestion, nausea, colic and digestive dysfunction (such as irritable bowel syndrome) because of its antispasmodic properties. In addition, it is thought to reduce colonic motility.

Peppermint oil is contraindicated for babies and young children as it can cause reflex apnoea or laryngospasm (Tester-Dalderup 1980, cited by Price and Price 2007). Caution is also suggested with high doses, which could cause sleep disturbance and skin irritation. A maximum of 3% is recommended for application to mucous membranes, and it is contraindicated in cardiac fibrillation (Tisserand and Balacs 1995).

Table 17
Peppermint essential oil in aromatherapy

System	Peppermint with
Respiratory (congestion, bronchitis, asthma)	*Eucalyptus* (cineole types), rosemary, sweet marjoram, clary sage, lavender, spike lavender, benzoin
Integumentary (itching, rashes, wound healing, eczema)	Lavender, bergamot, tea tree, patchouli, *Helichrysum*, myrrh, geranium
Digestive	Lavender, cardamom, citrus oils, black pepper, sweet marjoram, clove bud, coriander seed
Nervous (pain)	Lavender, *Ravensara aromatica*, nutmeg, clove bud

Mentha spicata – spearmint. This has a sweeter, warmer minty odour than peppermint (Williams 2000). The main chemical constituent is *l*-carvone at 50–70% (Lawless 1996). Carvone is a ketone that has two forms that are mirror images of each other. The *d*-carvone molecule has the odour of caraway, while the *l*-carvone molecule smells minty. Carvone is not toxic (Tisserand and Balacs 1995), so spearmint is thought to be a better option than peppermint for children (Lawless 1992). The indications are similar to peppermint; however, there would not appear to be the same amount of evidence to support this.

Mentha pulegium – pennyroyal. Pennyroyal essential oil contains between 55% and 95% of a ketone, *d*-pulegone. This is a very toxic ketone (hepatotoxic), and the high levels in pennyroyal oil render it unsafe for therapeutic use (Tisserand and Balacs 1995).

Ocimum basilicum – basil. The essential oils from several cultivars and chemotypes are available, e.g. Comoran (exotic basil), European basil, methyl chavicol and linalool chemotypes. *O. sanctum* is sacred basil, native to India. Basil essential oil is a colourless mobile liquid with a sweet, warm herbal, anisic odour. It is distilled from the leaves of the herb in Europe (mainly France), the Comoro Islands and Madagascar. The geographical influences (growing conditions) give rise to significant differences in the chemical compositions of the essential oils, despite the fact that they are derived from the same botanical species.

A constituent called estragole, also known as methyl chavicol, dominates Comoran basil. This belongs to a group of chemicals known as phenolic ethers. Estragole itself is not toxic, but is converted during its metabolism into a chemical, *1*-hydroxyestragol, that is carcinogenic and hepatotoxic. This is rapidly detoxified in the body, and basil oils with lower estragole contents are not a cause for concern. Comoran basil may contain between 40% and 87% estragole, up to 4% methyleugenol (genotoxic and carcinogenic), and up to 6% of the monoterpene alcohol linalool.

European basil oil is often referred to as the linalool chemotype, as the dominant constituent is linalool at up to 75%, along with estragole at up to 16.5% and methyleugenol, traces to 2% (Tisserand and Balacs 1995). Therefore, for use in aromatherapy, it is strongly recommended that the low estragole (i.e. <5%) be used.

Bowles (2003) suggests that methyl chavicol has antispasmodic qualities, and this is one of the properties attributed to basil essential oil (Lawless 1992, Price and Price 2007). These authors also state that basil is a 'tonic' (digestive and nervous systems), a stimulating oil with cephalic qualities. Therefore it can be of use in a variety of stress-related symptoms, e.g. muscular tension, headaches, poor concentration, nervous indigestion.

Table 18
Basil essential oil in aromatherapy

System	Basil with
Musculoskeletal (muscle tension, pain, stress related)	Lavender, rosemary, sweet marjoram, clary sage, black pepper
Nervous (stress, headaches, poor concentration, fatigue)	Lavender, rosemary, citrus oils
Digestive	Lavender, sweet marjoram, clary sage, citrus oils, sweet fennel, black pepper

Origanum majorana – sweet marjoram. Other species include *O. vulgare* or common oregano, which has many varieties, for example ssp. *O. glandulosum*, *O. virens* and *O. heracleoticum*. In aromatherapy practice it is important that therapists distinuish between sweet marjoram and the Thyme species commonly called marjoram – see *Thymus* (page 74).

Sweet marjoram essential oil is distilled from the dried flowering herb – the geographical sources include France,

Tunisia and Morocco (Lawless 1992). The essential oil has a warm, camphoraceous, herbal, spicy odour (Williams 2000). Chemically, it is characterised by monoterpenes (40%) and their alcohols (50%), notably myrcene, para-cymene, terpinen-4-ol and α-terpineol (Price and Price 2007). Myrcene, para-cymene, linalool and α-terpineol have all been attributed with analgesic properties (Bowles 2003); terpinen-4-ol may have diuretic properties (Baerheim Svendsen and Scheffer 1985). Marjoram is regarded as being of most use as an analgesic – especially for arthritic and muscular pain and rheumatism, and as a nervous sedative (Duraffourd 1982 cited by Price and Price 2007).

Table 19
Sweet marjoram essential oil in aromatherapy

System	Sweet marjoram with
Muscular (muscle tension, pain, spasm)	Lavender, lemongrass, basil, clary sage, black pepper
Articular (arthritis, joint pain)	Lavender, juniper berry, black pepper, grapefruit
Nervous (stress, anxiety)	Lavender, geranium, citrus oils

Pogostemon cablin – patchouli. Patchouli is a large, bushy perennial herb with a hairy appearance. It is closely associated with India, China and Malaysia – in the East it is widely used as a scent, where it also has a medical tradition of use (Lawless 1992). Patchouli essential oil is distilled from the leaves of the herb. Often these have been left to ferment slightly before drying then distilling. The fermentation process causes degradation of the plant material, so that the extraction of the volatile oil is enhanced and the yield greater. Patchouli essential oil has a clear amber appearance, is slightly viscous and has a rich, earthy, heavy and persistent odour.

The dominant constituents are the sesquiterpene alcohols – especially patchoulol (40%), according to Bowles (2003), and sesquiterpenes at up to 50%, including α- and β-bulnesene (Price and Price 2007). It is particularly useful for the skin – as it is both anti-inflammatory and cicatrising, it may be of support to the immune system, and it is one of the few essential oils cited as a phlebotonic (Price and Price 2007).

Table 20
Patchouli essential oil in aromatherapy

System	Patchouli with
Integumentary (acne, inflammation, eczema*)	Lavender, sandalwood, vetivert*, rose, geranium, citrus oils
Allergies	German chamomile
Nervous (stress, anxiety)	Lavender, rose, geranium, citrus oils (especially lime), sandalwood
Vascular	Lemon, cypress, geranium

* indicates a particular relationship between the condition and the oil

Rosmarinus officinalis – rosemary, of which many cultivars exist. Several chemotypes (essential oils derived from the same species but with different dominant chemicals) are available that have applications in aromatic medicine and aromatherapy – CT 1,8-cineole (Tunisia), CT verbenone (France) and CT camphor (Spain).

Rosemary is a strongly aromatic perennial shrub, whose flowering tops and leaves yield the essential oil. The oil has a strong, fresh, herbal, resinous, woody aroma (Williams 2000). The other dominant constituent is α-pinene; minor constituents are mostly monoterpenes and their alcohols and esters (Bowles 2003).

The most commonly cited uses for rosemary oil are as an analgesic, mucolytic and cephalic; Price and Price (2007) also state that it has 'neuromuscular action'. It is almost always described as a stimulating essential oil.

Table 21
Rosemary CT 1,8-cineole essential oil in aromatherapy

System	Rosemary with
Musculoskeletal (pain)	Lavender, marjoram, basil, juniper berry, lemongrass, black pepper
Nervous (pain, e.g. migraine or headaches, neuralgia)	Lavender, peppermint, clove bud
Debility, fatigue	Lavender, thyme, pine, basil
Respiratory (catarrh, congestion, bronchitis, coughs)	Thyme, *Eucalyptus* (cineole types), peppermint, Atlas cedarwood

There are a few authors who give conflicting information regarding the safety of rosemary essential oil – especially with regard to its uses in pregnancy and epilepsy (Price and Price 2007). Tisserand and Balacs (1995) suggest that oral doses are contraindicated in pregnancy, epilepsy and fever, and that the Tunisian 1,8-cineole CT should be used in aromatherapy practice as it has a lower camphor content (10–13% compared with 17–25% in the Spanish oil). For more detail, see Soulier (1996) and Mailhebiau *et al* (1996).

Salvia officinalis – 'Dalmatian' sage. There are many other species of sage that produce essential oil, including *S. sclarea* – clary sage (see below). Dalmatian sage essential oil is distilled from the leaves of the perennial herb, and has a strong, sweet, herbal, camphoraceous odour (Williams 2000). The essential oil contains α-thujone and β-thujone, neurotoxic ketones, at up to 50% and camphor, another neurotoxic ketone, at around 26% – not surprisingly, Tisserand and Balacs (1995) state 'the usual thujone content is sufficiently high to warrant its exclusion from aromatherapy'.

Salvia sclarea – clary sage. Clary sage is sometimes classed as a biennial herb, sometimes as a perennial; the essential oil is extracted from the flowering tops and leaves (Lawless 1995). It has very distinctive odour – sweet, warm, herbal and tea-like (Williams 2000). Chemically, it is complex, containing over 250 constituents. The dominant constituents are monoterpene alcohols, notably linalool at up to 26%, and esters, especially linalyl acetate at up to 75% (Price and Price 2007). These are also the dominant constituents of true lavender essential oil; for their characteristics, refer to page 61.

However, clary sage also contains an unusual constituent – sclareol – a diterpene alcohol (a larger molecule with twenty carbon atoms and two hydroxyl functional groups). Molecules of this size are not common in essential oils as they are often too big, and insufficiently volatile, to distil over in the essential oil. Sclareol is present at up to 7% (Price and Price 2007). Its molecular structure resembles oestradiol, and it has been suggested that this is responsible for its 'oestrogenic' effects (on the female reproductive system), although there is no evidence for this (Bowles 2003). It could also be possible that these effects are brought about via the limbic system.

Clary sage is an exceptionally useful essential oil. In addition to its potential therapeutic benefits to the female reproductive system (helping with irregular menstruation, painful menstruation, menopausal symptoms, perimenopause and PMS). It has antispasmodic, neurotonic and antidepressant actions, coupled with the ability to bring about a state of euphoria.

Table 22
Clary sage essential oil in aromatherapy

System	Clary sage with
Musculoskeletal (pain, spasm)	Lavender, Roman chamomile, juniper berry, lemongrass, black pepper, basil
Female reproductive	Geranium, rose, jasmine, sweet fennel
Nervous (debility, depression)	Lavender, geranium, rose, citrus oils, especially mandarin, sweet orange
Respiratory (asthma, spasm, coughs)	Lavender, bergamot

Clary sage essential oil is not toxic, and although some writers indicate that it is contraindicated in pregnancy, and it is not advisable either to consume alcohol or even drive if clary has been used, however there is absolutely no evidence to support these cautions.

The Thymes

The genus *Thymus* is botanically complex, with over 100 species and varieties or cultivars (Soulier 1995). Essential oils can be extracted from many species including *Thymus serpyllum* – wild thyme, *T. capitatus* – Spanish oreganum, *T. mastichina* – Spanish marjoram, *T. saturoides* – Moroccan thyme, *T. vulgaris* – common thyme and *T. zygis* – Spanish thyme.

In addition, several *T. vulgaris* chemotypes are available for use in aromatic medicine and aromatherapy, including CT thymol, carvacrol, linalool and geraniol. In general, from a safety point of view, oils with a high content of thymol and carvacrol (chemicals known as phenols) will be dermal irritants and strong mucous membrane irritants (Tisserand and Balacs 1995).

Thymus vulgaris – common thyme. Common thyme essential oil is distilled from the fresh or partially dried leaves and flowering tops of the perennial woody herb (Lawless 1995). The first distillate is red in colour and cloudy in appearance – this is termed 'red thyme oil'. This can be filtered and re-distilled to produce 'white thyme oil'. They both have a sharp, warm, herbal odour. If the chemotype is not specified, it is likely that the essential oil will contain up to 60% phenols, also para-cymene and γ–terpinene (monoterpenes) (Bowles 2003, Lawless 1995). Tisserand and Balacs (1995) give some detail regarding the chemistry of the thyme oils (see Table 23).

Table 23
Chemotypes of thyme

Chemotype	Thymol	Carvacrol
Thymol	32–63%	1–5%
Carvacrol	1–13%	23–44%
Thymol/carvacrol	26%	26%

From Tisserand and Balacs (1995)

Thyme oils should be used with caution on hypersensitive, diseased or damaged skin, or on children under two, and thyme should not be used at >1% concentration on mucous membranes (Tisserand and Balacs 1995). For this reason, they should not be evaporated.

Soulier (1995) gives much more detail regarding the chemistry of the thyme oils available for use in aromatherapy (see Table 24 for a summary). Price and Price (2007) provide indications and actions for seven thyme oils. All are credited with antimicrobial, warming, tonic and stimulant properties and some are antispasmodic and mucolytic.

The thyme oils have applications in many circumstances such as muscular aches and pains, debility, fatigue, respiratory congestion/coughs and low immunity. They all blend well with other herbal oils, and should be blended with non-irritant oils, especially lavender, rosemary and marjoram; also citrus (bergamot and lemon). Table 25 is a summary of the properties of the thymes according to Soulier (1995) and Price and Price (2007).

Table 24
Thyme oil chemistry

***Thymus vulgaris* – wild CT**	**Main chemical constituent(s)**
French, wild *Thymus vulgaris* low altitude	Thymol or carvacrol
French, wild *Thymus vulgaris* high altitude	Linalool
French, wild *Thymus vulgaris* high altitude, on exposed slopes	Geraniol (rare)
***Thymus* species**	
Thymus zygis (Spanish)	Thymol 50–75%
Thymus capitatus (Spanish oregano)	Carvacrol 70–85%
Thymus mastichina (Spanish marjoram)	1,8-cineole (60–75%) and linalool (5–20%)
Thymus saturoides (Morocco)	Borneol (15–30%)
Thymus serpyllum (mother of thyme)	Thymol – usually adulterated

Table 25
Thyme properties and indications

Species and chemotype	Properties and indications
Thymus mastichina	Catarrhal bronchitis, viral or bacterial infections
Thymus saturoides	Arthritis, fatigue, debility
Thymus vulgaris CT linalool	Very immunostimulant, fatigue, psychic and cerebral stimulant, anti-tussive, anti-infectious
Thymus vulgaris CT geraniol	Cardiotonic (Price and Price 2007)
Thymus vulgaris CT thymol	Bronchopulmonary, anti-infectious esp. chronic infections, anti-tussive, immunostimulant, mucolytic, warming

Lauraceae Family

This is a very large family of tropical and sub-tropical plants, containing over 2,000 trees and shrubs, many of which produce essential oils of commercial and medicinal significance.

Genus *Cinnamomum*

This genus contains around 200 species. From an essential oil and aromatherapy perspective, the most important are *Cinnamomum camphora* (camphor), *C. cassia* (cassia, Chinese cinnamon) and *C. verum* or *zeylanicum* (bark and leaf oils).

Cinnamomum camphora – camphor. Crude camphor exudes from the wood of the tall evergreen, via the fissures in the bark; the roots also contain the volatile oil. The essential oil is steam distilled from the crude camphor, rectified under vacuum producing three fractions – white (lightest), brown, and yellow camphor. Because of this, they are not classed as true essential oils as they are incomplete.

Only the white camphor has use in aromatherapy, as the safrole content of the other fractions is high, in brown camphor at 80% and 20% in yellow. Safrole is a very toxic compound, associated with genotoxicity and carcinogenicity (Tisserand and Balacs 1995). However, white camphor is dominated by the ketone known as camphor (30–50%) and 1,8-cineole (50%) (Tisserand and Balacs 1995).

The camphor content confers potential convulsant and neurotoxic hazards, so white camphor essential oil is contraindicated in epilepsy, fever, pregnancy and children under two (Tisserand and Balacs 1995).

Cinnamomum cassia – cassie (or cassia). Cassia is not used in aromatherapy as it is a strong dermal sensitiser and mucous membrane irritant. It contains very large amounts of cinnamaldehyde (75–90%) (Tisserand and Balacs 1995).

Cinnamomum verum (zeylanicum) yields two essential oils – one from its inner bark and one from the leaves. Cinnamon bark oil is not used in aromatherapy as it is a dermal irritant and strong dermal sensitiser, and mucous membrane irritant – mainly due to the eugenol content of up to 18% and cinnamaldehyde content of up to 75% (Tisserand and Balacs 1995).

Cinnamon leaf oil can be used in aromatherapy, although the

suggested maximum concentration is 3%. Tisserand and Balacs (1995) cite numerous oral contraindications related to the eugenol content. Eugenol is hepatotoxic and inhibits blood clotting. The leaf oil contains 70–90% eugenol and traces of safrole (<1%).

It is a yellow/brownish mobile liquid with a harsh spicy odour. Phenols generally are the most stimulating essential oil components. Because of its eugenol content, cinnamon leaf oil is rubefacient and antimicrobial.

In aromatherapy, Lawless (1995) suggests that it can be used to improve circulation, aid the digestive system, support the immune system and be of use in conditions such as debility and stress.

For further information, see Weiss (1997 and 2002).

Table 26
Cinnamon leaf essential oil in aromatherapy

System	Cinnamon leaf with
Cardiovascular (poor peripheral circulation)	Lavender, nutmeg, lemongrass, citrus oils, e.g. grapefruit
Musculoskeletal (aches and pains, rheumatism)	Lavender, nutmeg, rosewood, lemongrass, sweet orange
Digestive	Coriander seed, cardamom, palmarosa, sweet orange, mandarin
Nervous/immune (debility, stress-related conditions, susceptibility to infection)	Lavender, lemon, bay/laurel, rosewood, ylang ylang

Genus *Aniba*

This genus is closely related to *Cinnamomum* and many species produce essential oil. However, the most significant members of the genus *Aniba* are *A. duckei*, *A. parviflora* and *A. rosaeodora*, all of which yield rosewood, or bois de rose essential oil.

The most common species, from the aromatherapy essential oil trade perspective, would appear to be *A. rosaeodora* from Brazil. The essential oil is obtained from the wood chips from the tropical evergreen tree. There are environmental issues associated with its production (Santana *et al* 1997). The essential oil is a colourless mobile liquid with a mild, sweet, woody, floral odour (Lawless 1995).

Table 27
Rosewood essential oil in aromatherapy

System	Rosewood with
Nervous (stress, headaches, debility, etc.)	Lavender, bergamot, lemon, palmarosa, lemongrass, jasmine
Integumentary (including infections)	Lemongrass, lavender, palmarosa, geranium
Respiratory	Sandalwood, ginger, benzoin, lemon

According to Bowles (2003), rosewood contains linalool as its major component at 85.3%, followed by α-terpineol at 3.5% and cis-linalool oxide at 1.5%. The high linalool content could confer antimicrobial, analgesic and sedative properties to the essential oil. Price and Price (2007) highlight its applications as an antifungal for *Candida* and as an 'anti-infectious' agent for respiratory infections; also for its stimulating and tonic qualities that can aid in cases of general debility, overwork, sexual debility, nervous depression and stress-related headaches.

Genus *Laurus*

This genus is small. *L. nobilis* produces laurel essential oil, sometimes called bay laurel essential oil. This should not be confused with the bay essential oil from *Pimenta racemosa.* Bay laurel oil is obtained from the bay leaves. It is dominated by 1,8-cineole (30–36%) and it also contains phenols and linalool. According to Tisserand and Balacs (1995), it is a potential sensitiser and mucous membrane irritant. However, Schnaubelt (1999) suggests that it is most useful for lymphatic support during the treatment of upper respiratory tract infections – applied neat over the lymph nodes.

Genus *Litsea*

This is a fairly large genus; however, the most significant essential-oil producer is *L. cubeba (L. citrata).* A citral-rich essential oil is extracted from the fruits – may chang essential oil. China is the largest producer and consumer of this product. The essential oil is obtained from the small fruits (resembling cubeb pepper) of the small, fragrant tropical tree. The essential oil is a pale yellow mobile liquid with an intense, lemon, fresh-fruity odour (Weiss 1997). The oil is characterised by its high citral content (85%). Bowles (2003) cites may chang as containing geranial (40%), neral (33.8%) and limonene (8.3%). Geranial and neral are the isomers known in combination as 'citral'.

Citral can be irritating to the skin and mucous membranes, but it is also credited with calming, sedative properties according to Franchomme and Pénoël (1990 as cited in Bowles 2003).

Lawless (1995) suggests that may chang is useful for its antiseptic and deodorant qualities, that it is a digestive and stomachic, and a sedative that can combat tension and stress-related conditions. She also refers to 'recent research' that has shown that may chang can be of value in the treatment of cardiac arrhythmia, however, this is not referenced.

Table 28
May chang essential oil in aromatherapy

System	May chang with
Nervous (stress-related problems)	Lavender, rosewood, bergamot, palmarosa, geranium, rose, neroli or jasmine
Integumentary (excessive perspiration or odour)	Palmarosa, geranium, sandalwood
Digestive	Ginger, black pepper, mandarin

Genus *Ravensara*

This genus contains two essential-oil producers. *R. aromatica* yields an oil that is proving to be of great interest in aromatic medicine and aromatherapy. *R. anisata* also yields an essential oil (obtained from the bark of the tree), but this does not appear to have aromatherapy applications due to its notable constituents – estragole (88%) and *trans*-anethole (7%). It is thought that the essential oil would be carcinogenic and hepatotoxic (Tisserand and Balacs 1995).

Ravensara aromatica essential oil is distilled from the leaves and twigs of the large tree that is native to Madagascar. It is a colourless mobile liquid with a sweet, cineolic odour. According to Price and Price (1997), the main chemical constituent is the oxide, 1,8-cineole, with monoterpenes (including sabinene at up to 15%) and monoterpene alcohols (α–terpineol and terpinen-4-ol).

No contraindications are noted. Price and Price (1997) highlight its anti-infectious applications – for glandular fever, bronchitis, 'flu, sinusitis and whooping cough. It is also cited as an antiviral, useful for chicken pox, dendrites, herpes zoster, viral enteritis and viral hepatitis. Its actions on the respiratory system are enhanced by its expectorant property (probably due to the 1,8-cineole content). Schnaubelt (1998) suggests that it is a central nervous system tonic with uplifting qualities, making it a good choice in cases of 'flu. He also states that it is helpful for insomnia.

Table 29
***Ravensara aromatica* essential oil (Schnaubelt 1998)**

System	*Ravensara* with
Immune/respiratory (viral infections)	*Eucalyptus radiata* (50:50 topical application over thorax and inhalation)
Asthma	Inhalation, with lavender
Immune/herpes zoster (shingles)	50:50 with Tamanu fixed oil (*Calophylum inophyllum*) applied to lesions
Nervous (insomnia)	Osmanthus absolute

Genus *Sassafras*

This very small genus contains one species, *S. albidum*, which produces an essential oil. Sassafras essential oil is obtained from the dried root bark of the large deciduous tree. The essential oil contains 85–90% safrole and thus is not used in aromatherapy due to toxicity (carcinogenic).

Myristaceae Family

The family belongs to the order Magnoliales, and contains the large genus *Myristica*.

Genus *Myristica*

Generally, the *Myristica* are evergreen rainforest trees that produce yellow fleshy drupes. Only one is of major significance – *Myristica fragrans* – as the seed is the source of nutmeg, and the aril (the membrane around the seed) is the source of mace (Weiss 1997). Nutmeg and mace essential oils are widely used in the flavour and fragrance industries; they also have aromatherapy applications, however, nutmeg is more commonly used than mace.

Nutmeg essential oil is a pale yellow mobile liquid with a fresh, slightly piney top note and warm spicy middle notes (Williams 2000). It is dominated by monoterpenes – around 75% (Price and Price 1997). According to Bowles (2003), nutmeg is typically composed of α-pinene (22%), sabinene (18%) and β-pinene (15.6%) with terpinen-4-ol (7.9%) and the phenolic ether myristicin at 6%.

The predominance of monoterpenes may suggest that nutmeg essential oil is astringent, tonic and a mild rubefacient with analgesic potential. The presence of myristicin (and small amounts of elemicin) was at one time cited as conferring stupefying and psychotropic effects to nutmeg essential oil (Lawless 1992). However, the amounts used in Anglo-Saxon aromatherapy are too small to carry this risk. There are also traces of safrole and methyleugenol – both potentially carcinogenic. For this reason, Tisserand and Balacs (1995) suggest that it is better to use West Indian nutmeg in aromatherapy, as the East Indian oil contains more safrole (up to 3.3%).

Nutmeg essential oil is indicated as an analgesic, digestive stimulant and tonic (neurotonic, reproductive stimulant, uterotonic) (Price and Price 1997). They also cite Reynolds (1972) with reference to nutmeg (though it is not clear whether it is the essential oil) as an inhibitor of prostaglandin synthesis. For further information, see Tisserand and Balacs (1994).

Table 30
Nutmeg essential oil in aromatherapy

System	Nutmeg with
Nervous (pain – muscles, joints, rheumatic, neuralgia, sciatica, dysmenorrhoea.)	Lavender, ginger, black pepper, juniper berry, grapefruit, plai
Debility	Sandalwood, cardamom, jasmine or rose
Digestive	Ginger, coriander seed, cardamom, all citrus oils

Myrtaceae Family

From the aromatherapy perspective, this family is one of the most important. It is a large family, containing seventy-five genera and around 3000 species. Most members of the family are tropical trees and shrubs, indigenous to tropical regions of America, Asia and Australia.

Genera of interest to aromatherapists are *Syzigium* (formerly *Eugenia*), *Myrtus*, *Eucalyptus*, *Melaleuca*, *Leptospermum* and *Pimenta*.

Genus *Eucalyptus*

This is a very large genus. Most of the Eucalypts are indigenous to Australia; however, they are adaptable and have been introduced to many countries worldwide. Many Eucalypts yield essential oil from their leaves and twigs, most of which find applications in the pharmaceutical, flavour and fragrance industries. Many of the essential oils have aromatherapy applications.

The species that have most significance in aromatherapy and aromatic medicine – because of their expectorant and other properties, and high content of the oxide 1,8-cineole – are *Eucalyptus globulus* var. *globulus*, (blue gum), *E. polybractea* (blue-leaved mallee), *E. dives* (broad-leaved peppermint), *E. radiata* (narrow-leaved peppermint), *E. smithii* (gully-gum), and *E. viridis* var. *viridis* (green mallee).

The medicinal *eucalyptus* oils are often referred to as 'eucapharma oils' (Weiss 1997). *E. citriodora*, the lemon-scented gum, produces an essential oil with a characteristically high content of citronellal. This does not possess expectorant properties, but it is strongly antimicrobial, and it too has uses in aromatherapy.

E. staigeriana, the lemon-scented ironbark, is also being used in aromatherapy.

Eucalyptus globulus var. *globulus*, also known as *Eucalyptus* blue gum, is the most commonly available *eucalyptus* essential oil. The blue gum is grown for its timber as well as essential-oil production. It is grown in its native Tasmania and Southern Victoria; however, Spain, China and South America are also significant producers.

The essential oil is rectified, as the crude globulus oil has an unpleasant odour caused by lower aliphatic aldehydes that can also cause irritation and coughing when inhaled (Weiss 1997). There are standard specifications for globulus oil, published by the ISO and the BSI. According to these, the 1,8-cineole content should be 80–85%. Globulus oil is typically water white with a refreshing cineolic (*eucalyptus*-like) odour.

Eucalyptus globulus essential oil is therefore dominated by its oxide, which has been fairly well investigated with regard to safety and therapeutic actions. In large amounts, 1,8-cineole can have neurotropic effects (slurred speech, coma, convulsions), and it can cause respiratory irritation, as it is a rubefacient and mucous membrane irritant. Bowles (2003) cites Pénoël and Franchomme (1990), who suggest that *Eucalyptus globulus* should be used with care in asthma.

However, its therapeutic effects are considerable. 1,8-cineole is an expectorant, an anti-inflammatory in cases of bronchial asthma, and it may also be a stimulant of the trigeminal nerve – hence its ability to increase alertness (Bowles 2003).

Buchbauer (1993, 1996) states that 1,8-cineole can increase cerebral blood flow, and has also suggested that it has spasmolytic properties. Balacs (1997), in a comprehensive review of cineole-rich oils, explores the pharmacokinetics of 1,8-cineole, emphasising that this compound is absorbed very quickly from the air into the bloodstream.

Apart from 1,8-cineole, globulus oil contains significant amounts of α–pinene (up to 27%) and limonene (Bowles 2003 and Price and Price 1997).

Aromatherapy applications include a myriad of respiratory problems due to its expectorant and decongestant actions, including infections, bronchitis, sinusitis. It is also indicated for relief of muscular aches and pains, as an antiseptic for urinary tract infections and relief of migraine (Price and Price 1997). Pénoël (1992) suggests that globulus is particularly useful for all respiratory infections, especially 'deep' ones, 'flu, otitis, sinusitis and rhinitis, viral infections, lymphatic node infections, bacterial and fungal dermatitis and rheumatism.

Eucalyptus polybractea – the blue-leaved mallee. In its native Australia, the blue-leaved mallee is considered to be the most suitable species for large-scale production of *Eucalyptus* oil. The tree is of vital benefit to the local economy as it does not grow well elsewhere; it has a very high essential oil yield and a higher natural cineole content than *E. globulus* (thus an excellent natural source for isolating cineole), typically 70–90%.

Like globulus oil, it is usually rectified and the rectified oil has a sweet, cineolic, camphoraceous odour.

Other important constituents are p-cymene, terpinen-4-ol, α–pinene, limonene, β-pinene and sabinene (Weiss 1997).

E. dives – the broad-leaved peppermint. This essential oil has several chemotypes – 1,8-cineole, piperitone, and phellandrene. Interestingly, it is not cultivated in its native Australia. Price and Price (1997) give some information regarding the piperitone chemotype and its uses. They state that it contains 40–50% piperitone (a ketone) and 30% α–phellandrene. Although it is safe for 'normal' aromatherapy use, they suggest that it is contraindicated for babies and pregnant women, citing Franchomme and Pénoël (1990). Its main uses are for infections and wound healing, but the information is scant. However, they do comment that Beckstrom-Sternberg and Duke (1996) state that piperitone is anti-asthmatic and an insectifuge.

E. radiata – the narrow-leaved peppermint. This essential oil is widely used in aromatherapy, often in preference to other cineole-rich oils, as it would appear to have no associated hazards or contraindications. According to Weiss (1997), it is colourless to pale yellow with a fresh, powerful, peppery-camphoraceous odour; a 1,8-cineole content of up to 50% and phellandrene up to 40%. Price and Price (1997) emphasise its use as an energising oil for chronic fatigue and immune deficiency, but also as an expectorant/mucolytic, especially in combination with *E. smithii* (see below). They also suggest that it is important to blend it with a terpene-rich oil for best results – they do not give any suggestions but Scots pine would be appropriate. Pénoël (1992), in his article 'Winter Shield', gives a very different chemical composition from Weiss (1997) and Price and Price (1997) – giving an oxide content of 70%, and no mention of phellandrene. He suggests that radiata is useful for all respiratory infections (but not as 'deep' as discussed in relation to globulus), acne, vaginitis and endometriosis, and that it can be inhaled on its own or with rosemary.

E. smithii – the gully gum. This is an exceptionally useful cineole-rich oil. It is not cultivated in Australia, so the oil from Australia is obtained from wild trees. It is grown commercially in South Africa and Argentina. The 1,8-cineole content is 70–80%, and the rectified oil has a fresh cineolic scent (Weiss 1997). Price and Price (1997) cite properties and indications that are very similar to globulus, except that smithii also has 'balancing' qualities, and suggest that it is safe to use, undiluted, as a chest rub.

E. viridis var. *viridis* – the green mallee. This tends to co-exist with *E. polybractea* – they are very similar and often harvested indiscriminately. Weiss (1997) indicates that its 1,8-cineole content is around 80%, and that it is used in the same ways as *E. globulus.* In aromatherapy, it may be used in the same ways as other cineole-rich *eucalyptus* oils.

Table 31
Cineole-rich *Eucalyptus* essential oils in aromatherapy

System	*Eucalyptus* with
Respiratory (coughs, infections, sinusitis)	Lemon, thyme, rosemary, lavender, Scots pine, sandalwood
Musculoskeletal	Black pepper, lavender, basil, rosemary
Nervous (migraine, fatigue, debility)	Lemon, lavender

E. citriodora – the lemon-scented gum. This is very different from the *Eucalyptus* essential oils above in that it is not characterised by a high 1,8-cineole content. The essential oil is a colourless to pale yellow liquid with a strong, fresh, rosy-citronella odour; the ISO specification states that it should contain a minimum of 70% citronellal (Weiss 1997). Price and Price (1997) note that other significant constituents include its parent alcohol citronellol, isopulegol, and 1,8-cineole – although this can range from 0.4% to 17.9%.

Citronellal may have calming and antifungal properties (Bowles 2003), and Price and Price (1997) state that its bacteriostatic properties are due to a natural synergism between citronellal and citronellol, and that the oil is active against *Staphylococcus aureus.* They also claim that it has antifungal activity. Therefore, although this is not classed as a 'medicinal' essential oil, it may have considerable use in treating some infections, perhaps even MRSA.

E. staigeriana – the lemon-scented ironbark. Lemon-scented ironbark is now available for aromatherapy use, although its applications are not well documented.

According to Weiss (1997), the rectified essential oil is used in perfumery and toilet preparations. It has a sweet, fresh, fruity scent, and chemically it contains geraniol (9–18%), methyl geranate, geranyl acetate, limonene, β-phellandrene (12–34%) and neral.

If these constituents have the properties as described in Bowles (2003), it could be expected that this oil would be a useful antimicrobial (antibacterial and antifungal), analgesic (limonene and geraniol) and 'hormone balancing' (geraniol) agent in aromatherapy.

Genus *Leptospermum*

This is a fairly large genus containing around eighty species. Few of these are cultivated for their essential oils: perhaps because they lack viable quanties or the research is insufficient.

Leptospermum petersonii – lemon-scented tea tree. This is the source of a citral- and citronellal-rich essential oil that is used in perfumery, and occasionally in aromatherapy. Citral is isolated from the essential oil and used to produce the violet-scented chemical, ionone. *L. petersonii* essential oil has a lemony, pungent, diffusive odour. Aromatherapy uses are not well documented; however, it would be reasonable to assume that it has antimicrobial, sedative and possibly anti-inflammatory properties due to its aldehydes.

L. scoparium – manuka. Manuka essential oil has been investigated with regard to its antimicrobial properties and medicinal and pharmaceutical applications. It is distilled from the leaves and twigs of the tree, native to New Zealand.

It is chemically complex, and contains 15% leptospermone, a ketone, along with sesquiterpenes and their oxygenated derivatives (Price 1998). Leptospermone is a cyclic ketone that apparently inactivates hyalarodinase, an enzyme that increases diffusion of toxins in the tissues (a 'spreading factor'). It is postulated that leptospermone can act as an anti-venom-spreading agent, and also prevent the diffusion of toxins in the tissues due to infections (Merz 1994).

Price (1998) also states that manuka is an effective antiseptic and antifungal, with potential use against *Staphylococcus aureus*, including MRSA.

Genus *Melaleuca*

Often, members of the genus *Melaleuca* are referred to as 'paperbark trees', as typically the bark resembles paper and can be pulled off the tree in strips. Many members are essential-oil producers. The species of commercial importance and of significance in aromatherapy and aromatic medicine are *Melaleuca alternifolia* (tea tree), *M. cajuputi* (cajuput) and *M. quinquenervia* (niaouli). Essential oils from all three have been the subject of a considerable amount of research into their pharmaceutical and medicinal applications, and they are all used in aromatherapy. Other species of interest are *M. bracteata* (black tea tree) and *M. linariifolia.*

Melaleuca alternifolia is the source of tea tree essential oil. It is a small tree, native to Australia. The essential oil is extracted from the leaves and twigs, and is a colourless to pale yellow/green mobile liquid (Weiss 1997) with a distinctive, warm, spicy, slightly camphoraceous odour.

The essential oil is characterised by its terpinen-4-ol content – around 45% – and low 1,8-cineole content of 3–17% (Weiss 1997). Price (1998) comments that in the recent past, a 1,8-cineole content of a maximum of 4% was desirable, however many oils in fact have a 1,8-cineole content of nearer 15%. Bowles (2003) gives a figure of 3%, with the other significant constituents being γ– and α–terpinene at 15.7% and 7.1% respectively. Para-cymene is also present. It is usually noted for its analgesic potential, but here it may also be important in the antimicrobial/antifungal actions (Price and Price 1999).

Tea tree oil is a very useful antimicrobial. It has been well investigated in this respect, and as a consequence has become very popular in a wide range of antiseptic products. According to Carson and Riley (1995), cited in Bowles (2003), the constituents implicated here are terpinen-4-ol and α–terpineol. These two compounds usually occur together, sharing the same metabolic pathway. Budhiraja *et al* (1999) cited in Bowles (2003), suggest that terpinen-4-ol activates monocytes.

The medicinal odour of tea tree does restrict its popularity in aromatherapy, but it often forms part of aromatherapy support treatments. Price and Price (1999) ascribe analgesic, antibacterial, antifungal, antiviral, anti-inflammatory, and immunostimulant actions (among others) to tea tree essential oil. They suggest that it is most useful for treating many bacterial infections such as abscesses, acne, bronchitis, genito-urinary infections and MRSA (citing Carson, Hammer and Riley 1995, and Carson *et al* 1995), and for treating *Candida* infections. See also Williams *et al* (1998) and Caelli *et al* (2001).

When using tea tree for its antimicrobial actions, it can be blended with other essential oils that complement these, e.g. lavender and geranium (anti-inflammatory).

Melaleuca cajuputi – cajuput. Cajuput essential oil is mostly extracted from wild trees in Malaysia, Indonesia and Australia. There has been much confusion over its naming, thus literature is not always reliable – it has been frequently confused with *M. leucadendron* (Weiss 1997). The rectified product has a strong, camphoraceous, sweet odour (Williams 2000).

Chemically, the essential oil is variable. Bowles (2003) gives the botanical source of cajuput as *M. leucadendron*, and gives the main components as 1,8-cineole at 41.1%, α–

terpineol at 8.7% and para-cymene at 6%. Cajuput oil is used as a panacea in its countries of origin; in aromatherapy it is considered to be a useful antimicrobial, expectorant and analgesic, with applications in the treatment of respiratory and urinary tract infections, and for pain (Price and Price 2007).

M. quinquenervia – the five-veined paperbark. Native to Indonesia, New Caledonia and southern Papua New Guinea, it is the botanical source of niaouli essential oil. There are several chemovars, thus much variation in the chemical components of niaouli oil. Most of the essential oil is produced on the island of New Caledonia and then exported to France, where it is preferred to *Eucalyptus* oil (Weiss 1997). The essential oil is a colourless mobile liquid with a strong, sweet, camphoraceous odour (Williams 2000), not dissimilar to *Eucalyptus*.

Bowles (2003) gives the main constituents of niaouli from Madagascar as 1,8-cineole at 41.8%, viridiflorol (a sesquiterpene alcohol) at 18.1% and limonene at 5%.

In aromatherapy practice, niaouli is sometimes referred to as MVQ oil. In aromatic medicine in France, it is used for hepatitis and dysplasias of the colon, as a vaginal douche and to protect against radiation burns (Schnaubelt 1999). For Anglo-Saxon style aromatherapy, Schnaubelt (1999) suggests that it can be used topically as an expectorant, an anti-allergenic and anti-asthmatic. He also claims that it is an endocrine tonic.

Blending suggestions include tea tree, ravensara and the fixed oil of *Calophylum inophyllum* – apparently successful for haemorrhoids and genital herpes.

Genus *Myrtus*

Only one member of this genus is of importance – *Myrtus communis*, which yields myrtle essential oil. This should not be confused with the toxic essential oil of the wax myrtle (*Myrica* spp.).

Myrtus communis – myrtle. The essential oil comes from the fresh leaves of this evergreen shrub, which grows in the Mediterranean and North Africa (Weiss 1997). It is a yellow to orange or greenish mobile liquid with a warm, fresh and woody/camphoraceous odour.

Bowles (2003) gives the principal components of Spanish myrtle essential oil as myrtenyl acetate (35.9%), 1,8-cineole (29.9%) and α–pinene (8.1%) Myrtle oil is used in aromatherapy mainly for its expectorant qualities, where it can be of value in asthma, bronchitis, catarrh and chronic coughs. It also has applications for skincare, colds and 'flu (Lawless 1995). Schnaubelt (1999) suggests that it can be used with cypress in cases of pleurisy.

Table 32
Myrtle essential oil in aromatherapy

System	Myrtle with
Respiratory	Bergamot, lemon, lime, rosemary, ginger, cypress

Genus *Pimenta*

This comparatively small genus of aromatic shrubs and trees is indigenous to tropical regions of America and the Caribbean. Two species are commercially important, as their essential oils are used in the flavour and fragrance industry, but they are also available for use in aromatherapy. *Pimenta racemosa*, the bay rum tree, yields a leaf essential oil, and *P. dioica*, the source of allspice, yields pimento berry essential oil.

Pimenta racemosa – bay. This tropical evergreen tree is the botanical source of bay essential oil – often called West Indian bay, to avoid confusion with the essential oil from *Lauris nobilis*. The essential oil is obtained from the leaves; it is a yellow mobile liquid with a fresh, spicy, sweet odour (Williams 2000).

The main chemical constituents, according to Bowles (2003) are eugenol (56%), chavicol (estragole?) (21.6%) and myrcene (13%) – all well noted for their analgesic actions. However, Tisserand and Balacs (1995) suggest that the eugenol content would imply that the oil is a mucous membrane irritant, potentially hepatotoxic and that it could inhibit blood clotting. Therefore they contraindicate the oral use of bay oil in a range of situations where there is liver impairment or use of anticoagulants.

Topically, they suggest that the maximum concentration should be 3%, although they do note that West Indian bay was not in fact irritating to human skin at 10%.

In aromatherapy, bay oil is most often used as an analgesic for muscle and joint pains, neuralgia, and also for poor circulation. It blends very well with lime, grapefruit and lemon, ylang ylang, lavender, geranium and black pepper.

Pimenta dioica – pimento berry. Pimento berry (sometimes known as allspice) comes from an evergreen tree native to the West Indies and South America. It produces fruits that are steam distilled to yield a pale yellow mobile essential oil with a sweet, warm, spicy odour (Lawless 1995). Like bay essential oil (see above) it has a very high eugenol content – in the region of 60–95% (Tisserand and Balacs 1995). The same cautions apply.

Lawless (1992) gives a slightly different therapeutic profile. She highlights its uses for painful conditions affecting the muscles and joints, for poor circulation, chills, congested coughs, bronchitis and for nervous exhaustion.

Genus *Syzygium*

The clove was originally classified as *Eugenia caryophyllata*, and a revision of classification placed it in the genus Syzygium – it is now correctly referred to as *Syzygium aromaticum*. The clove is a spice of great commercial importance (historically and currently), as is clove bud oil (Weiss 1997). The essential oil also has aromatherapy and aromatic medicine applications, notably to relieve pain and assist the digestion.

Syzygium aromaticum – clove. Weiss (1997) gives a very detailed account of the clove, a tree indigenous to the Moluccas, whose buds became an enormously important spice. Clove products include the whole and ground buds that are used as a spice, clove bud oil, clove stem oil and clove leaf oil. The essential oils are also used as a source of eugenol for the pharmaceutical industry (Weiss 1997). In aromatherapy, only the clove bud oil is used, as the leaf and stem oils are considered to have too high a eugenol content to be safe (Lawless 1992).

Clove bud oil is a pale yellow mobile liquid with a warm, fruity, spicy odour (Williams 2000). Its principal chemical constituents are eugenol (76.6%), β-caryophyllene (9.8%) and eugenyl acetate (7.6%) (Bowles 2003). As you would expect, all the texts suggest that the essential oil is a powerful antibacterial and analgesic – certainly related to the eugenol content. So the same precautions given by Tisserand and Balacs (1999) for eugenol-rich oils apply to clove bud oil.

Price and Price (2007) suggest that clove bud oil is very useful as an analgesic for rheumatoid arthritis and neuralgia, as an antiseptic in many situations including abscess, acne, ulcers, wounds, as an anti-inflammatory and antispasmodic – especially for the digestive system – and for debility and fatigue, and as an immunostimulant.

Table 33
Clove bud essential oil in aromatherapy

System	Clove bud with
Musculoskeletal/nervous (pain)	Lavender, clary sage, bay, cinnamon leaf
Digestive	Sweet orange, lime, grapefruit, palmarosa
Nervous/immune	Rose or jasmine, lavender, bay, rosewood, ylang ylang, lime, benzoin resinoid, vanilla absolute

Piperaceae Family

Genus *Piper*

This family includes 10–12 genera and the genus *Piper* contains about 1000 species, many of which are tropical shrubs or woody climbers (Weiss 1997), although only one is of interest here.

P. nigrum – black pepper. Black pepper is native to the hills of Western India. Its history goes back to Ancient Greece and in the Middle Ages it was an extremely important commodity for the seasoning or preserving of meats and as a medicine. It is a perennial, woody, glabrous (devoid of surface hairs or projections) climber, according to Weiss (1997), with many greenish purple branches, alternate, ovate, shiny leaves and spikes of small yellowish green to whitish flowers. The dehiscent drupe contains a single seed, is green when unripe, becoming red when ripe and black on drying. The dried, black, wrinkled skin contains a single whitish seed, a peppercorn.

Black pepper oil is steam distilled from the imported unripe fruits, which have been dried and ground. The oil is colourless to pale green and fluid and the aroma, according to Lawless (1996), is 'fresh, dry-woody, warm and spicy'. The main components are terpenoid hydrocarbons (about 70–80%), including α-pinene, β-pinene and limonene, and the sesquiterpene, β-caryophyllene. The aroma is due largely to these components. Lawless (1996) suggests that the sesquiterpenes make up approximately 20–30% of the oil.

Price and Price (2007) state that it is analgesic, antibacterial, anticatarrhal, expectorant and febrifuge; and good for a sluggish digestion. It is useful for joint and muscle pain (being rubefacient), colds, 'flu and infections (Lawless, 1996). Traditionally it is also used for digestive complaints as diverse as diarrhoea, flatulence, colic, constipation, loss of appetite and nausea.

Table 34
Black pepper essential oil in aromatherapy

System	Black pepper with
Muscular	Lavender, basil, marjoram, rosemary, juniperberry, lemongrass, ginger, plai
Digestive	Clary sage, sweet fennel, citrus oils, ginger cinnamon leaf, , coriander seed, cardamom, peppermint
Respiratory	Frankincense, ginger, eucalyptus, rosemary

Poaceae Family

The family Poaceae was formerly known as the Gramineae. This is a fairly large family of monocots, and several genera yield essential oils of commercial importance (Weiss 1997) and of use in aromatherapy.

Genus *Cymbopogon*

The genus *Cymbopogon* (previously known as *Andropogon*) consists of between 50 and 60 species of tropical, perennial, tufted grasses, coarse-growing and with extremely aromatic foliage. The leaf oils used by aromatherapists are *C. nardus* (Ceylon citronella), *C. winterianus* (Java citronella), *C. citratus* (West Indian lemongrass) and *C. flexuosus* (East Indian lemongrass) and *C. martinii* (palmarosa). Lemongrass and palmarosa will be discussed below. In the genus *Vetiveria*, the only oil used by therapists comes from the rhizome and roots of *V. zizanioides.*

The oils all come from the Far East – India, Sri Lanka, Indonesia and Malaysia, and the oils are usually steam or hydro distilled (Weiss 1997).

Cymbopogon citratus – West Indian lemongrass. West Indian lemongrass is produced only under cultivation or through having been introduced. It is grown mainly in Argentina, Brazil, Guatemala, Honduras, Haiti and other Caribbean islands, Java, Vietnam, Malaysia, Sri Lanka, Madagascar and the Comoro islands, but also in the Philippines, China, India, Bangladesh, Burma, Thailand and Africa.

C. flexuosus – East Indian lemongrass. East Indian lemongrass is grown in Southern India, mainly in Kerala. There are two varieties – white stemmed and red stemmed – and it is usually the latter that produces the typical oil. Both have long narrow leaves and they rarely flower. Young leaves contain the most oil.

Generally, lemongrass essential oils are steam or hydro distilled and the leaves are allowed to wilt for two days prior to distillation in order to give a higher yield and increased citral content. They are also finely chopped prior to extraction (Lawless 1996). The oil has a strong lemony odour due to its high citral content and remains stable for a long time if correctly stored. The oil is usually a yellow to dark yellow or amber, slightly viscous, liquid. Table 35 shows the major constituents, although there is a great deal of variability.

Table 35
Major constituents of lemongrass essential oils

Component	*C. flexuosus*	*C. citratus*
Citral	85%	80%
Geraniol	5%	3%
Methyl heptenone	6%	0.3%
Myrcene	0.8%	20%
Dipentene	0	4%
Nerol	0	2%

The oil is fungicidal and potentially anticarcinogenic (Weiss, 1997). Lawless (1996) lists an impressive number of properties and suggests uses in skincare (acne, athlete's foot, excessive perspiration, scabies and as an insect repellent), for poor circulation, joint and muscle pain, for the digestive system (colitis, indigestion and gastro-enteritis), fevers and infectious diseases, headaches, nervous exhaustion and stress.

The high citral content should also suggest anti-inflammatory, sedative and antifungal properties (Franchomme and Pénoël 1990, Lis-Balchin 1995). Lawless (1996) suggests that it may cause dermal irritation or sensitisation in some and so should be used with care. This might be due to the high citral content but other components, such as monoterpenes, might mitigate against this (the 'quenching' effect).

Table 36
Lemongrass essential oil in aromatherapy

System	Lemongrass with
Integumentary (acne, athlete's foot and fungal infections)	Lavender, sandalwood, palmarosa, geranium, tea tree
Nervous (stress, anxiety)	Sandalwood, patchouli, vetivert, geranium, lavender, rose
Musculoskeletal (muscles/circulation, joint pain)	Sandalwood, juniper berry, black pepper, ginger, plai, basil

Cymbopogon martinii – palmarosa. Palmarosa essential oil is obtained from one of the two varieties of *Cymbopogon martinii*, or *C. martinii* var. *martinii* (motia), which grows in India. The closely related *C. martini* var. *sofia* is gingergrass; however, this oil is rarely used in aromatherapy.

Palmarosa essential oil is produced mainly from wild plants and has been known at least since the arrival of the Portuguese in India in the late sixteenth century. It is often the basis for cheap scents and soaps. It is produced by steam or hydro distillation of the fresh or dried grass (Weiss 1997).

The grass has many stiff stems of a yellow or greenish-yellow colour and the smooth leaves are long and narrow, and of a lighter green than the stems. Older leaves generally have a higher oil content than young ones.

The oil is pale yellow to olive with a sweet, floral, rosy, geranium-like aroma, but can vary greatly depending on origin, age or method of distillation.

The major components are monoterpene alcohols (geraniol (<95%), citronellol (<2%), linalool (<4%) and nerol) with some monoterpenes (limonene, myrcene, γ-terpinene), esters (geranyl acetate) and the sesquiterpene alcohol, elemol (Weiss 1997).

Lawless (1996) recommends it for skincare (acne, dermatitis, infections, sores and wrinkles). The geraniol content suggests that it would be a useful antifungal. Lawless (1996) cites Maury (1989) as testifying to its effect on the intestinal flora and therefore its usefulness in combating intestinal infections. She also recommends it for nervous exhaustion and stress.

Table 37
Palmarosa essential oil in aromatherapy

System	Palmarosa with
Integumentary	Lavender, geranium, sandalwood, patchouli
Nervous (stress)	Lavender, geranium, sandalwood
Immune	Lavender, rosewood, thyme geraniol or linalool

C. nardus – citronella. Citronella essential oil is noted for its aldehyde content and is grown mainly in Sri Lanka. *C. winterianus* is grown throughout the Far East, but now also in Central and South America.

The two types are generally known as Ceylon and Java types. The difference lies mainly in their geraniol content (see Table 38). For other differences see Weiss (1997).

Like the other members of this family, the oil comes from a tufted perennial grass with a fibrous root system, although in this case it is the leaves that are used. Prior to steam distillation they are usually wilted and chopped.

Lawless (1996) recommends it for skincare, the immune system and the nervous system. Schnaubelt (1998) again says that it is sedative (citral), anti-inflammatory and antispasmodic, while Bowles (2003) suggests that the geraniol content will contribute to an anti-infectious (antifungal), analgesic and sedative effect. The antifungal effect of geraniol might well be augmented by the presence of antifungal aldehydes.

Table 38
Comparisons of *C. nardus* and *C. winterianus*

Characteristic	*C. nardus*	*C. winterianus*
Colour	Yellow to brown/greenish yellow	Colourless to pale yellow
Aroma	Floral, woody, grassy, leafy – due to camphene-borneol-methyleugenol mix	Sweet, fresh and lemony
Main constituents	Geraniol (60%) Citronellal (15%) Citronellol (10%)	Geraniol (45%) Citronellal (50%) Citronellol (20%)
Uses	Insecticides, cheap perfumes and household cleaners and as raw material for geraniol, citonellol, citronellal and menthol production	Perfumes, toiletries and household cleaners and for the raw material as C. nardus

From Weiss (1997)

Genus *Vetiveria*

Vetiveria zizanioides – vetivert. Native to India, vetivert is used there and in other countries for soil conservation because of its extensive root mass. It is also used to make fans, mats, screens and thatch.

In Sri Lanka, vetivert is known as the 'oil of tranquility'. It is also produced commercially in China and some oil comes from Central America, the Caribbean and Brazil. Oil from wild plants is known as 'khus' in India. The best quality essential oil frequently comes from Réunion.

The stems and leaves are erect and develop from a branched and spongy rhizome. The leaves contain almost no oil and are usually burned before the roots are harvested.

The oil is produced by steam distillation from the roots and rhizome. The roots may be dried prior to distillation, as this usually causes an increased oil yield. Distillation may be by direct-fired stills and the roots may also be chopped and soaked in water prior to distillation.

Vetivert oil is dark brown to dark amber and viscous. Its odour is strong, sweet, woody and earthy. The odour is mainly influenced by α– and β-vetivone and khusimone. It contains mainly sesquiterpenoids, the major component being vetiverol (50–75%), although Price and Price (2007) put this component at much less.

Lawless (1996) lists its uses in skincare (acne, cuts, wounds and oily skin), for arthritis, muscular pain, rheumatism, sprains and stiffness, and for the nervous system (debility, depression, insomnia and nervous tension). Price and Price (2007) suggest that it is a good anti-infectious agent, a circulatory and glandular tonic, and an immunostimulant. They also state that it is emmenagogic, but cite no research to support this. Schnaubelt (1998) echoes this view of vetivert as a stimulant for the endocrine, immune and circulatory systems. Mojay (1996) suggests that vetivert can be used to treat eczema, and this may be due to its ketone and sesquiterpene content.

Table 39
Vetivert essential oil in aromatherapy

System	Vetivert with
Integumentary	Lavender, bergamot, geranium, patchouli, sandalwood
Nervous (stress)	Lavender, rose, sandalwood, violet leaf, ylang ylang
Musculoskeletal	Lavender, ginger, black pepper, lemongrass, plai
Immune	Lavender, palmarosa

Rosaceae Family

The family Rosaceae is very large indeed, comprising around 115 genera. However, one genus is of particular significance – the genus *Rosa.*

Genus *Rosa*

There are around 150 species of rose, and a myriad of named cultivars. Essential oils, concretes and absolutes may be produced from the flowers – all finding applications in the perfumery industry. The products vary in specification and odour, depending on the botanical source, geography and ecology, and method of extraction. Three species are recognised as being important for the fragrance industry –

Rosa damascena (the damask rose, common to Bulgaria and Turkey), *R. centifolia* (the cabbage or Provence rose) and *R. gallica* (known as the apothecary rose). These, and their hybrids, are extracted to produce essential oils, concretes and absolutes. Essential oils available for the aromatherapy profession include the most desirable Bulgarian and Turkish rose otto (essential oil distilled from *R. damascena*), rose oil from Morocco (essential oil distilled from *R. damascena*), rose oil from Morocco and France (essential oil distilled from *R. centifolia*), rose oil from Egypt (distilled from *R. gallica* var. *aegyptiaca*) and rose oil from China (essential oil from *R. rugosa* and others). Absolutes are also available for aromatherapy use – for example, Rose absolute centifolia, and Rose de Mai absolute, which originates from France and Morocco.

In aromatherapy, the most commonly cited properties attributed to rose essential oil are antibacterial, astringent, anti-inflammatory and cicatrisant actions, thus it is used to help the skin. Rose is also reputed to be of great assistance in problems pertaining to the female reproductive system, including PMS and menopause. The aroma is also thought to be antidepressant and an aphrodisiac. Rose hydrosol is used in skincare.

Chemically, the essential oil and absolutes are quite distinct. Rose essential oil is characterised by the presence of monoterpenes and their alcohols – geraniol (15.8–22.2%) and citronellol (22.5–60%) and small amounts of the aromatic alcohol phenyl ethanol (0.9–3%) (Price and Price 1999). The essential oil is colourless to pale yellow, with a deep, sweet, warm, rich, tenacious odour. The Moroccan (*R. centifolia*) oil is less spicy than the oils from Bulgaria or Turkey (Weiss 1997).

For information on rose absolutes, see Section 2.3 of this handbook.

Table 40
Rose essential oil in aromatherapy

System	Rose with
Integumentary (for mature, dry, oily or sensitve skin, eczema, thread veins)	Lavender, geranium, sandalwood, patchouli, vetivert, bergamot
Female reproductive	Clary sage, sweet fennel, cypress, juniper berry
Respiratory (hay fever, asthma, coughs)	Sandalwood, ginger, benzoin or peppermint, *Eucalyptus* (1,8-cineole types)

Rutaceae Family

Genus *Citrus*

The large family Rutaceae is divided into seven subfamilies – the subfamily Aurantioideae contains the Citreae, within which the most important genus from the fruit and volatile oil perspective is the genus *Citrus*. Oils obtained from this genus are widely used in the flavour and fragrance industries. Citrus has two sub-genera, containing sixteen sub-species.

The genus is very variable, with some large and some small trees, some having large fruit and some small. They are widely grown in Mediterranean Europe, but probably originated in tropical Eastern India. The only one to come from the Americas is grapefruit (Weiss 1997).

All are evergreen shrubs or small trees with fragrant flowers and leaves and edible fruits. The leaves are dotted with essential oil producing glands and, from some species, petitgrain oil is produced. The fruit oils are found in the flavedo (peel).

The peel oils are generally a by-product of the juice and canned fruit industry (the only exception to this is bitter orange) but small-scale extraction utilises cold expression. Most lemon and sweet orange oil is cold pressed, a process in which pressure is applied to the fruit, and oils and juice are drawn off simultaneously, but into separate channels. If oil is extracted prior to juice, then both abrasion and pressure are used. Lime is usually distilled, but distilled lemon and orange oils are rare (Weiss 1997).

The aroma of citrus oils comes mainly from aldehydes, but the oils also contain large amounts of terpenes. Some oils are deterpenated but these are not recommended for aromatherapy use. The distilled oils lack the furanocoumarin group of chemicals and therefore do not carry a phototoxic hazard, as do the cold-pressed oils (Tisserand and Balacs 1995).

In the genus, there are sixteen species and many more cultivars. Cold-pressed or distilled citrus fruit oils include sweet orange (*C. sinensis*), bitter orange (*C. aurantium*), lemon (*C. limon*), grapefruit (*C. paradisi*), mandarin (*C. reticulata*), bergamot (*C. aurantium* ssp. *bergamia*) and lime (*C. aurantifolia*).

The most significant essential oil obtained from citrus tree leaves is petitgrain oil, from *C. aurantium* ssp. *amara*, although other leaf oils are obtained from some other citrus species. The highly scented flowers of the bitter orange yield an essential oil known as neroli bigarade, obtained by distillation or by effleurage. This is widely used in perfumery. Neroli oil can also be obtained from the flowers of the sweet orange (neroli Portugal) and from lemon flowers (neroli citronier). Orange flower water is a distillation by-product that is indicated for oily skin. The flowers can be extracted with solvent, the product being an absolute – this is more correctly known as orange blossom absolute, not neroli.

All the citrus fruit oils, petitgrain and neroli oils have aromatherapy applications.

Generally, they are noted as being uplifting oils, with antibacterial activity and astringent action. They are often cited as being helpful to the digestion. Neroli oil is regarded to be one of the most calming oils, and is also widely used to help in cases of fragile, sensitive skin.

Because of the high percentage of monoterpenes in citrus oils they are prone to deterioration (Weiss 1997).

Citrus aurantifolia/C. latifolia – lime. Lime probably came from northern India and is widely grown there. It is a small tree with drooping branches and many short, stiff spines. The sharply scented flowers grow singly and the fruit is nearly spherical, small and greenish to light yellow in colour. Distillation is the usual method of extraction, although small amounts of expressed oil are available. Distilled oil is produced from both ripe and unripe fruits, while expressed oil comes mainly from green, unripe fruits.

Extraction can be by steam distilling the slurry from crushing whole limes and finely chopped peel or by distilling the juice from fruit pressing. Cold-pressed oil is more expensive.

Expressed oil is obtained by pressing whole fruits and passing the extract through centrifuges to separate the oil quickly. The manual method was to use an *écuelle à piquer* to scarify the fruit.

Components of the oil are extremely variable, but distilled oils have less citral, β-pinene and γ–terpinene, but more *p*-cymene, terpinen-4-ol and α–terpineol than expressed oil (Weiss 1997). Franchomme and Pénoël (1990) suggest that the expressed oil is composed of approx. 73% monoterpenes, with alcohols, esters, aldehydes (approx. 12%) and coumarins. Distilled oils do not contain coumarins, which can lead to increased oxidation risk, but pose no problems with phototoxicity.

Lawless (1996) cites uses in skincare (acne, brittle nails, boils, chilblains, cuts, greasy skin, herpes, insect bites, mouth ulcers and warts), for circulatory problems such as high blood pressure, varicose veins, nosebleeds and poor circulation, and for arthritis, cellulites, obesity and rheumatism. She recommends it for asthma, throat infections, bronchitis and catarrh, for dyspepsia, colds, 'flu, fever and infections. Franchomme and Pénoël (1990) state that it is sedative, anti-inflammatory, anticoagulant and antispasmodic and that it is useful for anxiety, stress, and also inflammatory and spasmodic problems of the digestive system. Table 41 (overleaf) provides a summary of the uses of lime essential oil.

Table 41
Lime essential oil in aromatherapy

System	Lime with
Integumentary	Lavender, bergamot, geranium, patchouli, sandalwood, vetivert
Nervous (stress)	Frankincense, sandalwood, ylang ylang, vetivert
Musculoskeletal	Lavender, bay, black pepper, lemongrass
Digestive	Coriander seed, cardamon, black pepper, ginger

C. limetta – sweet lime. Sweet lime is grown mainly in Southern Italy. It is very similar to lemon oil in aroma; only small volumes are produced.

C. aurantium ssp. *amara* – bitter orange. Bitter orange is native to South East Asia, but has now become established in the Mediterranean, especially Spain, hence the name Seville orange. The fragrant flowers produce neroli oil (*C. aurantium* ssp. *amara.* flos.); the leaves and twigs produce a petitgrain bigarade (*C. aurantium* ssp. *amara* fol.). The bitter orange tree is also spiny with aromatic leaves and flowers. The fruit is spherical, medium to dark green, becoming more yellow as it ripens.

The peel oil is darkish yellow and crystalline sediment may appear with age (Weiss 1997). The aroma is fresh and biting with sweet floral undertones. Major components include terpenes at approx. 90% (particularly δ-limonene), linalool, esters (linalyl acetate) and decanol. Due to the presence of furanocoumarins, this oil is considered phototoxic and limonene has been known to cause dermatitis in some individuals (Lawless 1996).

Lawless (1996) gives its uses as for sweet orange (see below) in the areas of skincare (oily skin and mouth ulcers), for obesity and fluid retention, bronchitis, chills, cold and 'flu, constipation, spasm of the digestive system, indigestion, palpitations, nervous tension and stress. Price and Price (2007) suggest that it is anti-inflammatory, anticoagulant, sedative and tonic, and recommend it for poor circulation, gastric pain, palpitations, constipation, anxiety and care of the gums.

The production of the leaf oil, 'petitgrain bigarade', became an established industry in Paraguay in the early nineteenth century (Weiss 1997). The main constituent of the leaf oil is the ester, linalyl acetate, but it also contains monoterpenes and 30–40% monoterpene alcohols (Franchomme and Pénoël 1990). Schnaubelt (1998) recommends this oil to balance the autonomic nervous system and Franchomme and Pénoël (1990) also support this, in addition to citing its antispasmodic, anti-inflammatory, anti-infectious and antibacterial properties. They suggest uses for rheumatism (of nervous origin), respiratory infections and infected acne and consider the oil to be without hazard.

The highly scented flowers of the bitter orange yield an essential oil known as neroli bigarade, obtained by distillation or by enfleurage. This is widely used in perfumery.

Neroli essential oil is regarded as one of the most calming oils, and is also widely used to help in cases of fragile, sensitive skin. It is a pale yellow liquid (that darkens when it deteriorates) with a sweet, spicy, orange blossom odour (Jouhar 1991). It must be kept cool and dark.

Chemically, neroli bigarade essential oil is dominated by linalool at 37.5%, with limonene at 16.6% and β-pinene at 11.8% (Bowles 2003). Linalool is antibacterial, analgesic, sedative and antispasmodic – all associated with the use of neroli in aromatherapy. Price and Price (1999) suggest that neroli bigarade is of most use as an antidepressant, lightly tranquillising and 'neurotonic' essential oil useful for fatigue, to aid sleep and to redress sympathetic nervous system imbalance. Weiss (1997) states that neroli bigarade is a weak antiseptic, but has strong bactericidal action against *Staphylococcus aureus*, and that in traditional medicine it was believed to induce a semi-trance state when inhaled warm.

Table 42
Neroli bigarade essential oil in aromatherapy

System	Neroli with
Musculoskeletal (muscular tension and spasm)	Lavender, ginger, black pepper, lemongrass
Integumentary (indicated for fragile or sensitive skin, acne, varicose veins)	Lavender, geranium, sandalwood, patchouli, bergamot, lemon
Nervous (nervous depression, anxiety, insomnia)	Lavender, geranium, vetivert, sandalwood, all citrus oils

C. aurantium ssp. *bergamia* – bergamot. Bergamot essential oil production became established in Italy in the sixteenth century and even today the most significant producer is Italy. The tree is similar to other citrus trees, the fruit being spherical and yellow when ripe.

According to Price and Price (2007), the major components are alcohols (45–60%) including linalool, esters (30–60%) including linalyl acetate, and monoterpenes including limonene, α– and β-pinene, and γ–terpinene, but again there is great variability (Weiss 1997).

This oil also contains phototoxic furanocoumarins, therefore care should be taken when using on the skin. It is interesting to note that 5-methoxypsoralen (5–MOP) is part of the UV treatment of psoriasis. A furanocoumarin-free essential oil is available, which effectively removes the risk.

Price and Price (2007) assign an impressive array of properties to this oil – it is antibacterial (monoterpenes), antiseptic, antispasmodic, antiviral (monoterpenes and aldehydes) and sedative (esters and aldehydes). They recommend Bergamot essential oil for wounds, herpes simplex (cold sores), insomnia, burns, loss of appetite and psoriasis. It is also indicated with German chamomile, lavender and sandalwood as a local wash for cystitis.

Lawless (1996) suggests uses in skincare (acne, boils, cold sores, eczema, as an insect repellent and for insect bites, oily skin, psoriasis, scabies, varicose ulcers and wounds). He also suggests bergamot essential oil for the respiratory system (halitosis, mouth infections, sore throat and tonsillitis), flatulence and loss of appetite, cystitis, leucorrhoea, pruritis and thrush, for colds, fever, 'flu and infectious diseases, and for anxiety, depression and stress.

Table 43
Bergamot essential oil in aromatherapy

System	Bergamot with
Integumentary	Lavender, geranium, patchouli, sandalwood, vetivert
Nervous (stress)	Frankincense, sandalwood, ylang ylang, vetivert
Musculoskeletal	Lavender, bay, black pepper, lemongrass, ginger
Digestive	Coriander seed, cardamom, black pepper, ginger
Genito-urinary	Sandalwood, juniper berry, lavender, German Chamomile, geranium

C. limon – lemon. This tree is from Asia, but the main producer of oils is now Sicily. The peel may be smooth or rough and the fruit is ovoid. The cold-pressed oil is clear, pale to greenish yellow (which turns brown with age) and the odour is fresh, sweet and lemony (Weiss 1997).

The major components of the oil are monoterpenes, at 90–95% (Price and Price 2007) and citral, the principal monoterpene being limonene (approx. 70%), but the main odour component is citral. The oil is also phototoxic (furanocoumarins) according to Lawless (1996) and may cause dermal irritation in some people. Price and Price (2007) state that it is anti-anaemic, antibacterial, antifungal (probably due to aldehydes), anti-infectious, anti-inflammatory and antiviral. It is astringent, diuretic and immunostimulant. *D*-limonene is thought to be anti-carcinogenic (Brudnak 2000).

Table 44
Lemon essential oil in aromatherapy

System	Lemon with
Integumentary	Lavender, bergamot, lime, geranium, ylang ylang, neroli, rose, jasmine, sandalwood, vetivert
Nervous (stress)	Frankincense, sandalwood, ylang ylang, geranium, rose
Musculoskeletal	Lavender, *Eucalyptus* (cineole types), black pepper, juniper berry, ginger, plai
Digestive	Coriander seed, cardamom, black pepper, ginger, sweet fennel
Respiratory	*Eucalyptus* (cineole types), sandalwood, ginger, basil

C. paradisi – grapefruit. Grapefruit is the only citrus species native to the New World and may be a cross of introduced plants on Barbados in the seventeenth century. The tree is large and vigorous with sturdy branches and angular twigs. It has large leaves and flowers, the latter being white and very fragrant. An essential oil is produced from the leaves. The fruit is large and light yellow to orange coloured (Weiss 1997).

Grapefruit essential oil is produced by steam distillation or cold expression of the fruits. The cold-pressed oil is yellow to pale orange/yellow, the aroma is sweet and fresh, similar to the fruit itself. It will deteriorate rapidly on exposure to the air (Weiss, 1997).

The major constituent of the peel oil is limonene (approx. 84%); nootkatone (a sesquiterpene ketone) and traces of a sulphur-containing compound give the oil its aroma. Monoterpenes make up about 95% of the oil (Weiss 1997). Lawless (1996) states that it is not phototoxic (although she cites furanocoumarins as present) and generally without hazard. Tisserand and Balacs (1995), however, suggest that a maximum level of grapefruit should be 4% due to its potential for phototoxicity, bearing in mind that this should be reduced if more than one phototoxic oil is used.

According to Lawless (1996), it is useful in skincare (acne, oily skin, toning the skin), cellulitis, obesity, stiffness and fluid retention, cold and 'flu, depression, headaches, nervous exhaustion and performance stress. Franchomme and Pénoël (1990) suggest that the oil is a good air antiseptic.

Table 45
Grapefruit essential oil in aromatherapy

System	Grapefruit with
Integumentary	Lavender, bergamot, geranium, ylang ylang, neroli, rose, jasmine, sandalwood, cypress
Nervous (stress)	Rosemary, ylang ylang, geranium, jasmine, neroli, palmarosa
Musculoskeletal	Lavender, *Eucalyptus* (cineole types), sweet fennel, black pepper, juniper berry, ginger, lemon
Digestive	Coriander seed, cardamom, black pepper, ginger, sweet fennel
Circulatory (lymphatic)	Sweet fennel, juniper berry, black pepper, rosemary, lemon

Harris (2005) cites Shen *et al* (2005), who demonstrated that the scent of grapefruit could affect autonomic nerve activity, increase lipolysis and metabolism, thus reducing weight in rats. These effects have not been reported in humans.

C. reticulata – mandarin. Mandarin and tangerine are usually considered as one species. Tangerine is used in English-speaking countries and mandarin elsewhere (Weiss 1997). The tree is normally small with a spreading habit and thin, drooping branches, with or without spines. The leaves are narrow and lanceolate. Mandarin petitgrain is produced by steam distillation of the leaves. Its main constituents are citral and linalool. The tree produces single white flowers and the fruit is a flattened sphere, with a peel that may vary from yellow to deep orange-red.

The peel oil is pale to mid yellow or orange depending on the cultivar, and the aroma is intense, sweet and, very occasionally, not very pleasant – a faint fishy note may be present. The major constituents are usually monoterpenes (limonene 65%+), alcohols (including linalool), aldehydes at around 1% (short-chain fatty aldehydes), trace amounts of thymol and anthranilates (Price and Price 2007). Thymol and dimethyl anthranilate contribute to the aroma (Weiss 1997).

Lawless (1996) recommends mandarin essential oil for skincare, notably acne, oily skin, scars, stretch marks and as a 'toner', for fluid retention and obesity, for digestive problems and the nervous system (insomnia, nervous tension and restlessness). She considers it useful for children and pregnant women, as it carries little hazard, and she states that it blends well with other citrus oils, especially neroli, and spice oils.

Price and Price (2007) consider it to be antifungal,

antispasmodic, anti epileptic and hepatic. They highlight its calming quality and its applications in cases of insomnia and nervous tension. Tisserand and Balacs (1995) consider it to be without hazard, but Franchomme and Pénoël (1990) suggest that it does contain furanocoumarins and therefore is phototoxic.

Table 46
Mandarin essential oil in aromatherapy

System	Mandarin with
Integumentary	Lavender, geranium, neroli, rose, frankincense
Nervous (stress)	Lavender, geranium, neroli
Digestive	Coriander seed, cardamom, black pepper, ginger, sweet fennel, marjoram
Circulatory (lymphatic)	Sweet fennel, juniper berry, black pepper, rosemary, grapefruit

C. sinensis – sweet orange. Sweet orange is probably a native of the Southwest China–Burma borders, but now is grown throughout the world. It is medium-sized tree with ovate, glossy green leaves. The branches may be spiny. Sweet orange petitgrain oil is produced by distilling the leaves, with monoterpenes the main constituents. Flowers are white, fragrant and occur singly or in clusters. The yellow-orange fruit is oval or ellipsoidal with a smooth peel.

The oil is produced by cold pressing peel or whole fruit or by steam distilling the residues from segmenting or juicing (Weiss 1997). Cold-pressed orange is pale yellow-orange to dark orange, but colours do vary according to the cultivar used and the country in which it is grown. The aroma is fresh, fruity and similar to the peel when scarified.

The main constituents are monoterpenes (approx. 90%), mainly limonene, and the aldehydes octanal and decanal, alcohols (mostly linalool) and esters – octyl and neryl acetates (Weiss 1997). Franchomme and Pénoël (1990) also include furanocoumarins and ketones (β-carvone and α–ionone) and suggest that the oil may be phototoxic. They recommend it for dyspepsia, insomnia, anxiety and as an air disinfectant.

Hongratanaworakit & Buchbauer (2007) suggest that both pharmacological and psychological effects can be active simultaneously. In their investigation into the effects of transdermal absorption of sweet orange oil (while preventing the subjects from smelling the oil), they found that autonomic arousal was decreased, but the subjects actually felt more cheerful and vigorous at the same time. They concluded that their research was evidence to support the use of sweet orange oil for the relief of depression and stress.

Lawless (1996) cites the uses as for bitter orange (see above) and suggests that it blends well with lavender, neroli, lemon, clary sage, and spice oils. She considers it to be non-hazardous.

Table 47 (overleaf) provides a summary of the uses of sweet and bitter orange essential oils in aromatherapy.

Table 47
Sweet and bitter orange essential oils in aromatherapy

System	Orange with
Digestive	Sweet fennel, marjoram, clary sage, coriander seed, cardamom, black pepper, ginger
Nervous (stress)	Jasmine, geranium, neroli, sandalwood
Circulatory (lymphatic)	Sweet fennel, juniper berry, black pepper, rosemary, grapefruit

Santalaceae Family

This family belongs to the order Santalales. The Santalaceae is the sandalwood family; it contains around twenty-five to thirty genera – however, classification is difficult. The genus of interest, genus *Santalum*, contains sixteen to twenty tropical, evergreen, parasitic trees and shrubs (Weiss 1997).

Genus *Santalum*

The most important species is *Santalum album* ('East Indian sandalwood'), which is prized for its wood as well as the essential oil. The use of both can be traced back over 2500 years in India. Sandalwood essential oil has a very important place in perfumery (East and West). *Santalum album* is a small evergreen tree, described as an obligate root parasite that becomes less dependent on its host as it matures. The volatile oil is contained in the heartwood and the larger roots, and the essential oil is obtained by hydro or steam distilling the pulverised heartwood and major roots.

Sandalwood harvesting is officially controlled in India; however, sandalwood oil is also produced in Australia, from *S. spicatum* and *S. austrocaledonicum*. West Indian sandalwood is not true sandalwood – the oil is obtained from *Amyris balsamifera* (Weiss 1997).

East Indian sandalwood essential oil is a pale yellow, viscous liquid, with a soft, sweet, woody, animalic, balsamic odour (Weiss 1997). According to Bowles (2003), the main chemical constituents are sesquiterpene alcohols – α–santalols (50%) and β-santalols (25%). East Indian sandalwood is currently very scarce and is often substituted with western-Australian sandalwood in aromatherapy practice, despite the differences in odour and chemistry. In a review of sandalwood oils, Erligmann (2001) does attempt to differientate between the two speicies from a therapeutic perspective, claiming that *S. spicatum* is perhaps a more powerful antiseptic and antiflammatory oil.

S. spicatum has a soft, woody, extremely tenacious, balsamic, sweet odour with a dry spicy resinous top note (Valder *et al* 2003). It contains over seventy constituents and, like *S. album*, is predominated by sesquiterpenes. Chiral GC analysis of β-bisabolols could potentially be used to differentiate between the two essential oils.

True sandalwood essential oil is one of the most useful oils in aromatherapy. It is used for its tonic and sedative qualities; it is antiseptic, it is said to have diuretic qualities and to be helpful to the urinary system, and also to be a bronchial dilator, thus helping the respiratory system (Holmes 1994/5, Price and Price 2007).

In a study exploring the self-perceived effects of sandlewood (used as a fragrance), Sheen and Stevens (2001) found that the predominant effect was calming, and users reported a sense of being 'able to manage' and general well-being. The effects were related to temporal factors and could be modified by the individual's conscious choice. This corroborates, to a large extent, the findings of Holmes (1997) using the Fragrance Energetics model.

Table 48
Sandalwood essential oil in aromatherapy

System	Sandalwood with
Musculoskeletal (pain, spasm)	Juniper berry, lemongrass, black pepper, clove bud, ginger
Nervous (debility, anxiety, depression)	Rose, jasmine, geranium, benzoin, patchouli, rosewood, bergamot, sweet orange
Respiratory (asthma, spasm, coughs, congestion)	Bergamot, ginger, benzoin, Atlas cedarwood
Urinary (cystitis, urinary tract infection)	Juniper berry, bergamot

Zingiberaceae Family

This family includes around forty-seven genera of about 1500 species of perennial tropical and subtropical herbs (Weiss 2002). There are two subfamilies: the Costoideae and the Zingiberoideae. Ginger (*Zingiber officinale*), plai (*Z. cassumunar*) and cardamom (*Elettaria cardamomum*) belong to the latter.

Genus *Zingiber*

Zingiber cassumunar – plai. Plai essential oil is a recent introduction to the West, but has been used for some time by Thai massage therapists. It is used primarily for joint and muscle complaints.

The plant is native to Thailand, Indonesia and India and the oil is steam distilled from the fresh rhizome. It has a cool, green, peppery, tea-tree-like aroma. The main active components are sabinene (25–45%), γ–terpinene, α–terpinene, terpinen-4-ol (25–45%) and trans-1-(3,4-dimethoxyphenyl) butadiene (1–10%) (Price and Price 2007).

Wells (2003) attributes numerous properties to this oil and cites research (Pongprayoon 1997), into its anti-inflammatory action, and its ability to reduce oedema and pain for up to eighteen hours using a dilution of 10%. A 10% blend has also been used for post-operative swelling after knee surgery. He suggests that it has a cooling action on inflammation and may, in conjunction with tarragon or rosemary and cypress, reduce the intensity of an asthmatic attack induced by exercise or allergy. He also recommends it for IBS and menstrual cramps. He records no adverse reactions.

Price and Price (2007) note that it has been suggested for use in Myalic Encephalopathy (ME) and for pain relief; however, it is perhaps its anti-inflammatory potential that is most significant – they cite research by the Thailand Institute of Scientific and Technological Research, Chatochak, which demonstrated that trans-1-(3,4- dimethoxyphenyl) butadiene was twice as potent as Diclofenac (Voltarol).

Table 49
Plai essential oil in aromatherapy

System	Plai with
Digestive (IBS)	Black pepper, orange, tarragon[1], mandarin, cardamom
Articular	Black pepper, lemon neroli, Himalayan cedarwood, orange, nutmeg, lemon
Respiratory: asthma	Tarragon, rosemary and cypress
Female reproductive (menstrual cramps)	Linden blossom, sweet marjoram, orange
Immune (ME)	May chang, ho wood, Spanish lavender

[1] Tarragon is considered to be toxic and should not be used in aromatherapy (Tisserand and Balacs)

Zingiber officinale – ginger. Ginger is native to tropical India and South East Asia, Australia and Japan. It has an ancient use as a spice, being mentioned in the earliest Sanskrit literature and in writings in China. It was also used by the ancient Middle Eastern cultures and was introduced to the New World by the Portuguese.

It is an erect, leafy perennial with purple flowers, growing from a horizontal rhizome near the surface of the soil. The rhizome is firm with a corky and scaly skin and varies in colour from buff to dark brown through to black.

The oil-containing cells are scattered throughout the cortex and the pith of the rhizome. The oil is obtained by distilling the preferably unpeeled, dried and powdered rhizomes. Its main constituents are sesquiterpenes (zingiberene at <40%, α-curcumene at <20%, farnesene at <9%) and sesquiterpene alcohols (<18%). Monoterpenes (1–20%) and aldehydes influence the aroma (Weiss 2002).

The oil is a pale yellow to orange mobile liquid, becoming more viscous with age or exposure to the air. The aroma is rich, warm and spicy. In perfumery, ginger is used as a 'toner' and its odour is very difficult to imitate (Jouhar 1991).

Ginger essential oil is an analgesic, general tonic, digestive tonic and expectorant (Price and Price 2007). Franchomme and Pénoël (1990) suggest that it is anti-inflammatory, a bronchodilator and antipyretic. It is indicated for digestive pain, chronic bronchitis and flatulence, and as a general tonic.

Table 50 (overleaf) provides a summary of the uses of ginger essential oil in aromatherapy.

Table 50
Ginger essential oil in aromatherapy

System	Ginger with
Digestive	Sweet fennel, marjoram, clary sage, coriander seed, cardamom, black pepper, palmarosa, all citrus oils, especially sweet orange and mandarin
Nervous (fatigue, debility)	Jasmine, geranium, neroli, sandalwood, frankincense, rosewood, lime
Musculoskeletal (tension, pain)	Lavender, lemongrass, clove bud or cinnamon leaf, black pepper, plai, grapefruit, Atlas cedarwood

Genus *Elettaria*

Elettaria cardamomum – cardamom. Cardamom also has an ancient history as a spice – reference to it has been found on a clay tablet from ancient Sumaria. The major producer is India (Weiss 2002).

It is a strong perennial herb growing from a rhizome as ginger does, but producing dark green, lanceolate leaves and pale green flowers in panicles. The fruit is a spherical, pale green to yellow, trilocular capsule containing an essential oil mainly in the dark brown seeds. The fruits are sun-dried, or dried in a flue, to avoid mould forming. The oil may also be distilled from fresh fruits and CO_2 extraction is possible (Weiss 2002).

The essential oil is colourless to pale yellow with a warm and spicy aroma, with an added camphoraceous or cineolic note (Weiss 2002). The major constituents of the distilled oil are 1,8-cineole (around 50%), and α–terpinyl acetate (24%) and limonene (6%) (Bowles 2003).

Lawless (1996) states that its main uses are for the digestive system (anorexia, colic, cramp, dyspepsia, flatulence, halitosis, heartburn, indigestion and vomiting) and the nervous system (mental fatigue and nervous strain). Franchomme and Pénoël (1990) state that it is tonic and stimulating, antispasmodic, anticatarrhal and expectorant – probably because of the high 1,8-cineole content. They also suggest that it is a weak and variable anti-infectious and antibacterial agent.

Table 51
Cardamom essential oil in aromatherapy

System	Cardamom with
Digestive	Coriander seed, black pepper, ginger, plai, cinnamon leaf, clove bud, all citrus oils, especially sweet orange and mandarin
Nervous (fatigue, debility)	Jasmine, ylang ylang, rose, sandalwood, bergamot, frankincense, rosewood
Respiratory	Lavender, Atlas cedarwood, bergamot, sandalwood

Section 2.2
The Gymnospermae

In the previous section, the essential oils studied all belonged to the Class Angiospermae – the flowering plants. Now, we will look at essential oils from the Class Gymnospermae.

It is thought that the first aromatic plants appeared on the planet 300 million years ago. These were the coniferous trees. Some of these species continue to thrive today; many are notable sources of essential oils, such as species of *Pinus* (pine), *Picea* (spruce), *Abies* (fir) and *Cupressus* (cypress).

The Coniferales is the largest order of Gymnosperms and the most widely distributed. Most of its 49 genera are evergreen trees and contain around 570 species. There are six families: Araucariaceae, Cephalotaxaceae, Cupressaceae, Pinaceae, Podocarpaceae and Taxodiaceae. These trees generally grow at high altitude in northern latitudes, most showing a pyramidal growth pattern, with simple leaves, needles or scales. Most are monoecious (having the female and male reproductive organs separated in different structures on the same plant) and produce pollen grains.

The Coniferales includes several families containing aromatic genera. The Pinaceae and Cupressaceae families include genera that are notable for the production of essential oils used in aromatherapy.

Cupressaceae Family

This family contains many species that produce essential oils, several of which have aromatherapy applications, and a few of which are toxic. The genera of interest to aromatherapists are Thuja (Arbor vitae), Chamaecyparis, Cupressus (true cypress) and Juniperus (juniper).

Thuja occidentalis – thuja (also known as 'cedar' or 'tree of life'). Despite its long herbal tradition, thuja essential oil is considered too toxic to have applications in aromatherapy as it is dominated by a ketone, thujone (60%) (Lawless 1996). Thujone is one of the ketones that may cause convulsions and produce liver and CNS damage; even small doses can result in nausea, hallucinations and coordination difficulty (Bowles 2003).

Chamaecyparis obtusa – Hinoki false cypress. There are no documented accounts of the therapeutic use of its essential oil.

Cupressus sempervirens – Mediterranean cypress. This is a tall evergreen tree with graceful, slender branches and a conical shape, which bears small flowers and round, brownish grey cones. There are many species of cypress, but it is mainly *C. sempervirens* that is of interest to aromatherapists.

In aromatherapy, this is the most commonly used true cypress essential oil and it is produced in France, Spain, Croatia and Morocco from the needles and twigs. It is a pale yellow to green/olive mobile liquid with a lingering, smoky, balsamic odour.

Chemically, it is dominated by α-pinene, delta-3-carene and cedrol (Bowles 2003) i.e. it has both monoterpenes and a sesquiterpenol as major constituents. Price and Price (2007) give a full profile of this chemically complex oil, suggesting many uses in aromatherapy. They highlight its usefulness as a neurotonic for debility and also as a phlebotonic with astringent action, making it useful for broken capillaries. Other areas of application include the respiratory system, the urinary system (diuretic) and the skin (astringent).

Schnaubelt (1999) suggests that cypress has antispasmodic properties and is therefore indicated for all bronchial complaints. He also concurs with Price and Price (2007) regarding its efficacy as a venous and lymphatic decongestant, aiding oedema and varicose veins.

Table 52
Mediterranean cypress essential oil in aromatherapy

System	Cypress with
Respiratory (bronchitis, pleurisy*) (Schnaubelt 1999)	Sandalwood, Eucalyptus spp. (1,8-cineole types), myrtle*, frankincense, bergamot
Lymphatic/circulation (varicose veins, oedema)	Patchouli, geranium, juniper berry, rosemary, lemon, grapefruit, sweet fennel
Integumentary (broken capillaries, oily skin, acne)	Ylang ylang, geranium, rose, neroli, bergamot, sandalwood

* indicates a particular relationship between the condition and the oil

Genus *Juniperus*

Several essential oils are obtained from the genus *Juniperus* and applications common to this group of essential oils are for pain, the respiratory and urinary systems, and as depuratives and diuretics.

Juniperus ashei – Mexican cedar. Despite its name, this tree is not a true cedar. The essential oil obtained from *J. ashei* is also called Texas cedarwood oil, as it is here that the essential oil is distilled. It is dominated by cedrene and cedrol (Lawless 1996) and can be irritating to the skin. The main aromatherapy applications are for articular pain, respiratory congestion and urinary tract infections (Lawless 1996). However, Bowles (2003) states that Texan cedar oil is obtained from *J. mexicana*, and contains thujopsene, a sesquiterpene, at 32%.

Juniperus communis – juniper. Juniper essential oil is widely used in aromatherapy practice. The essential oil for aromatherapy use is obtained from the berries (although 'inferior' oil is extracted from the needles and twigs) and it is produced in Italy, France and Croatia. It is a colourless or pale green mobile liquid with a fresh, resinous, woody aroma. The needle/twig product has a turpentine note.

Chemically, the dominant constituent is α–pinene at 33%. Myrcene, a monoterpene said to have analgesic properties, is present at around 11%; β-farnesene – a sesquiterpene with potential pheromonal effects (Bowles 2003) – is present too at 10.5%. Terpinen-4-ol and α–terpineol are also present – these are said to have diuretic action.

Price and Price (2007) cite several uses for juniper berry

essential oil, most of which are echoed in popular aromatherapy books. These include its applications for muscle and joint pain (including gout), because of its analgesic, rubefacient and depurative qualities. It is also antiseptic, depurative and diuretic and so can aid problems such as cystitis, oedema and cellulite, as well as acne and weeping eczema.

Table 53
Juniper berry essential oil in aromatherapy

System	Juniper berry with
Urinary	Sandalwood, bergamot, grapefruit
Lymphatic/circulation (cellulite oedema)	Sweet fennel, geranium, cypress, rosemary, lemon, grapefruit, sage, black pepper
Musculoskeletal (muscular and articular aches and pains, gout)	Rosemary, sweet marjoram, basil, black pepper, grapefruit, plai, lemongrass

Juniperus oxycedrus – medlar. A rectified essential oil, known as cade oil, is obtained from *J. oxycedrus.* Cade oil is an ingredient of some pharmaceutical preparations for skin disorders, such as psoriasis, and it is also used in the fragrance industry. It is used in aromatherapy, but not widely, due to a reputation for causing sensitisation reactions (Lawless 1996).

Juniperus sabina – savin, juniper or shrubby red cedar. The essential oil is known as savin oil. It is not used in aromatherapy, as it is embryotoxic (Tisserand and Balacs

1995), due to its high content of sabinyl acetate, and irritating to the skin. In addition, it has an unpleasant odour (Lawless 1996).

Juniperus virginiana – Virginian cedar. Virginian cedarwood essential oil is used widely in the fragrance industry. It is also commonly used in aromatherapy. However, it is often named 'cedarwood' and thus confused with Atlas cedarwood essential oil.

The commonly cited uses are very similar, except that it is not recommended in pregnancy (Lawless 1996). Virginian cedarwood has a smell reminiscent of pencil shavings. Its dominant constituents are cedrol (26%), α–cedrene (24.5%) and thujopsene (15%).

Pinaceae Family

In this family, the four most important genera, from the essential oil perspective, are Pinus (pine), Picea (spruce), Abies (fir) and Cedrus (cedar).

The essential oils are produced in the resin canals of the trees, and can be extracted from the wood, the needles and the cones. Essential oils from the family Pinaceae are widely used in the flavour and fragrance industry, and in pharmaceutical preparations. The essential oils are also used in various antiseptic products and disinfectants.

In aromatherapy, the main applications of the pine essential oils are to aid the respiratory system (especially if infection is present), to aid convalescence and to help in cases of general debility. The pine oils are used as analgesics for articular and muscular pain, and are also indicated in cases of infections of the urinary system.

Spruce and fir oils are less frequently used; their principal application is to aid the respiratory system.

Essential oils from the true cedars are also applied to aid the respiratory system and to alleviate muscular and articular pain. In addition, they may be used to help with skin problems, and are considered to be very effective at reducing stress.

Genus *Pinus*

Pinus mugo var. *pumilio* – the dwarf pine. The essential oil is extracted from the needles and twigs of the tree. It can be irritating as it contains delta-3-carene at 35% (Bowles 2003), and is thus largely avoided in aromatherapy due to the potential for irritation (Lawless 1996).

Pinus palustris – longleaf pine. This tree produces an oleoresin (turpentine) that is steam distilled and rectified to yield a product also known as turpentine. The wood of the tree can be steam distilled to yield the essential oil, which is used in aromatherapy (Lawless 1996).

Pinus sylvestris – Scots pine. The essential oil is steam distilled from the needles of the tree. In aromatherapy, this is probably the most commonly used of the pine oils. The essential oil is produced in Hungary, Siberia and the Balkans. It is a colourless/pale yellow mobile liquid with a strong, coniferous, fresh odour.

The essential oil is dominated by monoterpenes, notably α–

(42%) and β-pinene and delta-3-carene at 20.5% (Bowles 2003). These constituents are said to be mucolytic (Franchomme and Pénoël 1990); but may also be irritating to the respiratory tract, according to Bowles (2003). However, perhaps this is why they have the effect of making mucus thinner, as they may stimulate the goblet cells of the respiratory tract. Bowles (2003) also suggests that such monoterpene-rich essential oils should be used with caution on those who suffer from asthma.

The same constituents are said to be rubefacient and therefore analgesic, hence their use for muscle and joint pain.

Schnaubelt (1999) suggests that Scots pine is an endocrine stimulant containing 'hormone-mimicking, polycyclic terpenoids' and is a 'forceful tonic and adrenal stimulant' that can be used at 10% over the kidney/adrenal area for adrenal support.

Table 54
Scots pine essential oil in aromatherapy

System	Scots pine with
Respiratory (especially colds, 'flu, rhinitis, sinusitis)	Cypress, Atlas cedarwood, rosemary, marjoram, lemon, galbanum
Musculoskeletal (muscular and /or joint pain)	Juniper berry, rosemary, black pepper, marjoram, lavender
Nervous/immune/endocrine (adrenal support, stress, debility, convalescence)	Basil, rosemary, lemon, grapefruit, lavender, black pepper

Genus *Picea*

Picea mariana – black spruce. Information on its uses is scarce, however Schnaubelt (1999) suggests that it is a bronchial decongestant and an even more powerful adrenal stimulant than *P. sylvestris.* It can be combined successfully with Scots pine and blackcurrant absolute in cases of adrenal exhaustion (Schnaubelt 1999).

Picea alba – white spruce. It is not used in aromatherapy practice.

Picea excelsa – Norway spruce. It is not used in aromatherapy practice.

Genus *Abies* (the true firs)

The fir oils are not widely used in aromatherapy practice, although they are used extensively in the fragrance industry. They are dominated by monoterpenes.

Abies alba – silver fir. The essential oil is a pale/colourless mobile liquid with a pleasant, sweet balsamic odour. It contains santene, the pinenes, limonene and bornyl acetate (an ester). Its aromatherapy applications are for the respiratory, musculoskeletal and immune systems (Lawless 1996).

Abies balsamifera – Canadian balsam fir. According to Bowles (2003), this essential oil typically contains α-pinene at 33%, delta-3-carene at 21.5% and bornyl acetate at 11.9%. These constituents would suggest that Canadian fir has similar applications to the other coniferous oils; Lawless (1996) suggests that it may be used in skincare (burns, cuts and bruises), respiratory conditions, cystitis and depression.

Abies siberica – Siberian fir. There is no reliable information on its use in aromatherapy.

Genus *Cedrus* (the true cedars)

Cedrus atlantica – Atlas cedar. Atlas cedar is the most commonly used true cedarwood essential oil. This is a tall evergreen tree with a highly aromatic hard wood, native to the Atlas Mountains of Algeria. It has close relations with *C. deodora* (Himalayan cedarwood) and *C. libani* (Lebanese cedarwood). Atlas cedarwood essential oil is from Morocco, extracted from the woodchips and sawdust. It is a pale amber, slightly viscous, liquid with a woody, warm, camphoraceous odour.

It is dominated by sesquiterpenes (cedrene at 50%), sesquiterpene alcohols at 30% (atlantol and cedrol) and ketones at 20% (α–atlantone and γ–atlantone). Price and Price (2007) highlight its applications as an antiseptic for skin problems (scalp and eczema), for the urinary tract, and as an antipruritic when combined with bergamot. They also recommend it as a lymphatic stimulant (cellulite is an indication) and as a mucolytic with applications for the respiratory system. Schnaubelt (1999) suggests that it is a gentle but powerful circulatory stimulant and also useful for fluid retention and helpful for cellulite.

In France, Atlas cedar is contraindicated in pregnancy and for children (Price and Price 2007); however, its external use in Anglo-Saxon style aromatherapy does not appear to carry a risk (Tisserand and Balacs 1995).

Table 55
Atlas cedarwood essential oil in aromatherapy

System	Atlas cedarwood with
Respiratory (bronchitis)	Sandalwood, *Eucalyptus* spp. (1,8-cineole types), benzoin resinoid, ginger, frankincense
Integumentary – scalp (seborrhoea, stimulant)	Juniper berry, rosemary, lavender, ylang ylang, bergamot
Integumentary (eczema, itching, pruritis)	Sandalwood, vetivert, bergamot, lavender
Lymphatic/circulation	Sweet fennel, juniper berry, rosemary, grapefruit, lavender, black pepper

Cedrus deodora – Himalayan cedar. It produces a very similar essential oil to the Atlas cedar (Lawless 1996).

Section 2.3
The Absolutes and Resinoids of Aromatherapy

Absolutes and resinoids are produced for the perfumery industry; therefore most do not have a tradition of therapeutic use, certainly not in the way that essential oils have. With the possible exceptions of jasmine, rose and neroli absolutes and benzoin resinoid (rose and neroli are also available as essential oils), few absolutes and resinoids have even acquired an aromatherapy tradition of use. They are not used in aromatic medicine.

Concretes, absolutes and resinoids are products of solvent extraction, as essential oils are products of distillation, enfleurage or expression. Solvent extraction can be used to remove the odourous component from any aromatic material. However, solvent extraction is generally used for those parts of plants whose volatile oils would extensively degraded by distillation, e.g. jasmine and tuberose. The final residue of the process is usually a viscous, reddish-brown coloured liquid. The colour depends on the pigments in the plant material. Some absolutes are decolourised with activated charcoal, which absorbs some of the pigments.

The absolutes are the most highly concentrated and unaltered aromatic materials for use in perfumery and aromatherapy. The equipment for solvent extraction is costly. The solvent can influence the odour of the product slightly, but despite this solvent extracted oils are considered to be closer in odour to the natural plant than their steam-distilled counterparts. Traces of solvent may remain in the absolute, and it is for this reason that only high quality absolutes should be used in aromatherapy practice. In general, it is advisable to use only one absolute in a blend; their powerful odours in combination can often smell like a strong, cheap perfume!

Some absolutes and resinoids may have physiological actions, and most appear to exert effects on the psyche. Their highly concentrated odours mean that they are used in very low concentrations, so any therapeutic effects will probably be due to inhalation and via the limbic system rather than on a direct pharmacological level.

Absolutes and resinoids that have been used in Anglo-Saxon aromatherapy practice include:

- benzoin resinoid – some therapeutic effects on the skin and respiratory system; mainly used for its calming, comforting odour
- hyacinth – no known pharmacological effects, useful for mental stress and fatigue, apathy, depression, negative state of mind, and to enhance creativity
- jasmine – does have aromatherapy tradition of use – mainly for the nervous system, childbirth and skincare. It has an uplifting, stimulating odour
- narcissus – no known pharmacological effects; it is narcotic, aphrodisiac, sedative
- neroli/orange blossom absolute – this is also available as an essential oil; it has an aromatherapy tradition of use in skincare and for reducing anxiety
- osmanthus – fairly new ingredient in skincare formulations – it may enhance collagen formation.

Warren and Warrenburg (1993) demonstrated that it could create a positive, happy frame of mind

- rose – the essential oil is traditionally used in aromatherapy for skin and female reproductive system. It is also useful for combating anxiety and depression. The absolute is also widely used
- tuberose – no known pharmacological effects; narcotic effects
- vanilla – no known pharmacological effects; sedative and anxiolytic, possibly an appetite suppressant
- violet leaf – has been used in aromatherapy for skincare and pain; mainly used for nervous exhaustion, headaches and insomnia

Agavaceae Family

Genus *Polyanthes*

The most significant species in this family is *Polyanthes tuberosa*, which yields tuberose essential oil (extracted by enfleurage) or an absolute from its flowers. Tuberose is a tall perennial with lily-like flowers – the double flower variety is used as a cut flower. Tuberose absolute is an expensive product that is widely used in perfumery. The absolute is a soft, dark brown paste with a heavy, sweet, floral aroma. Chemically, it is very complex, containing alcohols (nerol, farnesol, geraniol and benzyl alcohol), aromatic esters, eugenol and tuberone, a ketone. This absolute has narcotic properties. In Anglo-Saxon aromatherapy, it is used mainly for its fragrance and to promote relaxation and sleep. For further information, see Lind (1998).

Amaryllidaceae Family

Genus *Narcissus*

This genus contains *N. jonquilla* (jonquil) and *N. poeticus* (narcissus), from which an absolute can be obtained. Narcissus absolute is used in aromatherapy, and it has many applications in perfumes. It is a dark orange/olive green viscous liquid with a heavy, sweet, herbaceous, hay-like, earthy, floral odour. It only smells like narcissus on extreme dilution. Like all absolutes, it is chemically very complex, containing aromatic esters and eugenol. Linalool is present and there are trace amounts of indole. Indole (a cyclic imine) itself smells of mothballs, but it is faecal at 10% and jasmine-like in trace amounts (Williams 2000). According to Lawless (1992, 1995), it has antispasmodic, aphrodisiac and narcotic actions but can be used in aromatherapy for its fragrance alone.

Caryophyllaceae Family

There is only one genus relevant to perfumery or aromatherapy studies – the genus *Dianthus*, which contains *Dianthus caryophylius* (carnation) and *Dianthus plumarius* (pink).

Carnation absolute has been used in aromatherapy, and is of importance in perfumery. It has a very powerful fragrance and is extremely costly to produce (Jouhar 1991).

Liliaceae Family

This family contains, amongst others, onions, chives, leeks, garlic, (all genus *Allium*) bluebells, lilies and hyacinths. Essential oils of garlic (and onion, etc.) are obtainable, and these oils do have many uses in the flavour industry. They also have clinical and pharmaceutical significance, but are not normally used in aromatherapy because of their pungent odours.

Genus *Hyacinthus*

Hyacinthus orientalis – hyacinth. Hyacinth has been used in aromatherapy as well as the fragrance industry for which it is produced. It is cultivated commercially in both Holland and France. The absolute is a dark, greenish liquid that has a very powerful, sharp, green, leaf-like odour, only pleasant on dilution, and only resembling hyacinth on extreme dilution (Jouhar 1991).

Chemically, it is complex, dominated by phenolic alcohols (e.g. phenyl ethanol), eugenol and aromatic esters (e.g. benzyl acetate). There is very little to support any claims of pharmacological effects such as antiseptic, styptic and sedative (Lawless 1995 and Rose 1999), however, its odour is said to be narcotic, uplifting, refreshing, invigorating and it may enhance creativity. In a study by Warren and Warrenburg (1993), hyacinth fragrance evoked happiness, sensuality, relaxation and stimulation while decreasing feelings of apathy, irritation, stress and depression.

Oleaceae Family

The Oleaceae belong to the order Schrophulariales. The most important genera to study, from the essential oil and aromatherapy perspectives, are the genus *Jasminum* and the genus *Osmanthus.*

Genus *Jasminum*

There are over forty species, but only three are cultivated specifically for essential oil, concrete and absolute production – *Jasminum auriculatum* (mainly cultivated in India), *J. grandiflorum* (known as Spanish jasmine, cultivated in India, and France/the Mediterranean) and *J. sambac* (the most commonly cultivated jasmine in India). There are also many cultivars. In some plantations, *J. grandiflorum* is grafted on to the sturdier, wild *J. officinale.*

This is a fascinating genus to study for many reasons, ranging from botanical, geographical and ecological through to the essential oil and absolute production, its aesthetic and clinical uses to its distinctive and celebrated fragrance. Jasmine absolute is a dark, orange/brown liquid. The aroma varies according to its source, but is typically floral, fruity, heavy and animalic with a waxy, spicy dry out (Williams 2000).

It is dominated by aromatic esters such as benzyl acetate, methyl jasmonate and benzyl benzoate. Indole, a cyclic imine (nitrogen-containing compound) is present – if pure, this has a 'mothballs' odour; it is faecal at 10% and jasmine-like at less than 1% (Williams 1996 and 2000).

Jasmine has a long historical tradition as an aphrodisiac. In Anglo-Saxon aromatherapy, its main uses are for counteracting depression, stress and lack of confidence. For more information see Lawless (1995) and Holmes (1998).

Hirsch *et al* (2007) demonstrated that the aroma of jasmine could dramatically improve bowling scores, and suggest that mechanisms may be by regulating mood, enhancing alertness, reducing anxiety while improving self-confidence and not least improving hand-eye coordination. They concluded that a similar effect could be expected in other activities that involve hand-eye coordination and precision.

Table 56
Jasmine absolute in aromatherapy

System	Jasmine with
Integumentary (for mature skin, dry, oily or sensitive skin)	Lavender, geranium, sandalwood, patchouli, violet leaf
Musculoskeletal (muscular stress/tension)	Lavender, lemongrass, black pepper, ginger, Roman/German chamomile, clary sage
Nervous (depression, tension, stress, fatigue, lethargy)	Sandalwood, ginger, cardamom

Genus *Osmanthus*

This genus of evergreen shrubs and small trees has one species, *Osmanthus fragrans*, whose flowers are extracted to produce an absolute that has become increasingly popular in perfumery. This evergreen shrub is native to the Himalayas, Japan and China, where the powerfully scented flowers are used to scent tea. Osmanthus fragrance has been investigated in relation to its effects on mood (Warren and Warrenburg 1993), and this research would indicate that it has a role to play in aromatherapy. Osmanthus absolute has a distinctive odour; it is reminiscent of plums and raisins (Leffingwell 2000), and apricot (Warren and Warrenburg 1993).

The absolute contains linalool and linalool oxide, and other constituents include phenolic alcohols, acids and ionones. Warren and Warrenburg (1993) found that osmanthus fragrance's 'stimulating and happy qualities are further supported by prominent reductions in the negative moods of apathy and depression'. It has been suggested that osmanthus may also enhance collagen formation, soothe skin sensitivity and help restore and refine the skin (Leffingwell 2000) – hence its recent inclusion in commercial skincare products.

Orchidaceae Family

Genus *Vanilla*

There are three species that yield vanilla as a product – Bourbon or Réunion vanilla is obtained by extraction from *Vanilla planifolia* Andrews, Tahiti vanilla is obtained from *Vanilla tahitensis* Moore, and West Indian vanilla from *Vanilla pompona*. Vanilla is a perennial herbaceous vine that produces large white flowers followed by green capsule-like fruits – pods – that are harvested while immature. The pods are cured and treated by solvent extraction to yield a resinoid and absolute. Vanilla absolute is a brown viscous liquid with the characteristic sweet, rich odour of vanilla. It is chemically very complex. Vanillin, a phenolic aldehyde, is present at around 2% (Klimes and Lamparsky 1976, Jouhar 1991).

Although vanilla is widely used as food flavouring and in perfumery, its applications in aromatherapy are not well documented. It is used mainly as a balsamic agent and for its soothing odour. It blends well with floral essential oils and absolutes (ylang ylang, geranium, rose and jasmine), sandalwood and the spice oils (ginger, clove and cinnamon).

Rosaceae Family

Please also refer to Section 2.1 for information on the genus *Rosa* and rose essential oil.

Genus *Rosa*

Rose absolutes are orange-yellow to orange-brown viscous liquids. The absolutes from Morocco and France are known as 'Rose de Mai' absolutes. The absolutes have much greater amounts of phenyl ethanol than the essential oils – around 60% (Tisserand and Balacs 1995).

Table 57
Rose absolute in aromatherapy

System	Rose absolute with
Nervous (depression, anxiety, debility)	Lavender, geranium, sandalwood, cardamom, benzoin, patchouli, bergamot and citrus essential oils
Female reproductive (PMS – irritabilty, mood swings, etc.)	Clary sage, bergamot, geranium, Roman chamomile

Rutaceae Family

Please refer to Section 2.1 for information on the Rutaceae and the essential oils of the genus *Citrus.*

Citrus aurantium var. *amara* – bitter orange. The flowers of the bitter orange can be extracted with solvent, the product being an absolute – this is known as orange blossom absolute, not neroli.

Orange blossom absolute is a dark, orange-brown viscous liquid with a warm, rich, tenacious odour – similar to the flower itself – and is of great value in perfumery. Chemically, it is also dominated by linalool (32%) and linalyl acetate (16.8%); it also contains nerolidol and farnesol (sesquiterpene alcohols associated with anti-cancer effects (Bowles 2003) at around 7%, phenyl ethanol (4.5%) and methyl anthranilate, a nitrogen-containing ester, (3.0%) (Weiss 1997).

In aromatherapy, it is used in the same way as neroli.

Table 58
Orange blossom absolute in aromatherapy

System	Orange blossom absolute with
Integumentary (indicated for fragile or sensitive skin, acne, varicose veins)	Lavender, geranium, sandalwood, patchouli, bergamot, lemon
Nervous (nervous depression, anxiety, insomnia)	Lavender, geranium, vetivert, sandalwood, all citrus oils
Musculoskeletal (muscular tension and spasm)	Lavender, ginger, black pepper, lemongrass

Styraceae Family

The only genus of importance for essential oil studies is the genus *Styrax*.

Genus *Styrax*

There are several members of this genus that exude aromatic balsamic resins if the trunk is cut or damaged. Resinoids may be produced from the resin by solvent extraction. *Styrax benzoin*, *S. paralleloneuris* and *S. tonkinensis* are tall trees native to tropical Asia. Two types of product are obtained, depending on the geographical and botanical origins. Siam benzoin is produced from *S. benzoin* and *S. tonkinensis* trees that grow in Laos, Vietnam, Cambodia, China and Thailand; Sumatra benzoin is produced from *S. benzoin* and *S. paralleloneuris* trees growing in Sumatra, Java and Malaysia (Lawless 1992).

The resinoid is brown in colour, viscous, with a sweet, balsamic, vanilla-like odour. The main chemical constituents are coniferyl cinnamate (an ester) in Sumatra benzoin, and coniferyl benzoate (also an ester) in Siam benzoin (Lawless 1995). Both contain traces of the aromatic aldehyde, vanillin, which contributes to the sweet, vanilla-like odour.

As it is not an essential oil (the odorous molecules are not sufficiently volatile to distil over), it is disregarded by many authors. However, benzoin resinoid has many well-established areas of use, e.g. in pharmaceutical preparations for the gums and skin, as a component of tinctures to aid the respiratory system, in perfumery and also in aromatherapy, where it is primarily used for its calming, comforting scent, for stress-related problems, for skin problems and respiratory problems (Lawless 1996).

It is advisable to prepare a 'carrier' oil containing benzoin, to which other essential oils can be added. The carrier should be of known concentration and decanted after the resinous material has precipitated. If the resinoid is added directly to a blend for massage, the preparation will be sticky, and leave the skin feeling sticky too.

Table 59
Benzoin resinoid in aromatherapy

System	Benzoin with
Nervous (stress, debility, anxiety, depression)	Rose, jasmine, sandalwood
Respiratory (asthma, spasm, coughs, congestion)	Bergamot, ginger, sandalwood, frankincense
Integumentary (inflammation and irritation, wounds)	Myrrh, patchouli, lavender, *Helichrysum*

Tiliaceae Family

Tilea vulgaris – linden. This tree bears clusters of strongly scented flowers that have a long herbal tradition. A concrete and absolute may be obtained from the flowers – the absolute is used in perfumery, and occasionally in aromatherapy, usually for headache and nervous tension.

Violaceae Family

Viola alba is the Parma violet, *V. odorata* is the sweet violet and *V. suavis* is the Russian violet. The violet, a small tender perennial plant, is cultivated in southern France for production of a concrete and absolute from the fresh leaves and flowers. These are used in perfumery and flavouring confectionery. The leaf absolute has 'an intense, rather unattractive, green and peppery odour' (Jouhar 1991).

It is chemically complex – 2-trans-6-cis-nonadien-1-al is the component largely responsible for the odour – containing n-hexanal, n-octen-2-ol-1, benzyl alcohol and others, and traces of eugenol (The International School of Aromatherapy 1993).

Absolutes of *V. alba* and *V. odorata* are available for aromatherapy use. The main indications for the use of violet leaf absolute are in skincare, stress, insomnia, and headache (Lawless 1995).

Table 60
Violet leaf absolute in aromatherapy

System	Violet leaf with
Integumentary (indicated for fragile or sensitive skin, eczema acne, thread veins)	Lavender, geranium, sandalwood, patchouli, bergamot, vetivert
Nervous system (dizziness, headache, insomnia)	Lavender, clary sage, basil, hyacinth

Glossary

abortifacient induces abortion.

absolute a highly concentrated aromatic extract obtained by alcoholic extraction of the concrete, which is acquired by the process of solvent extraction (or enfleurage) of aromatic plant material.

analgesic pain relieving.

annual a plant whose life cycle is completed within one growing season.

anthelmintic a remedy that destroys intestinal worms.

antibacterial destroys and/or inhibits bacterial growth.

anticoagulant inhibits the coagulation of blood.

antidepressant counteracts depression.

antifungal destroys and/or inhibits fungal growth.

antiphlogistic counteracts inflammation.

antipruritic relieves itching.

antisclerotic prevents the hardening of tissue.

antiseborrhoeic restrains sebum production.

antispasmodic relieves spasm in smooth muscle tissue, includes skeletal muscle.

antitussive relieves coughing.

antiviral destroys viruses.

anxiolytic reduces anxiety.

aril the membrane covering a seed.

aromachology the study of the psychological effects of odours.

aromatherapy the therapeutic application of essential oils and aromatic plant extracts in a holistic context, to maintain or improve physical, emotional and mental well-being.

aromatic medicine the application of essential oils in the medical field, as developed and practiced in France, by medically qualified persons.

aromatology the intensive, clinical use of essential oils to treat disorders.

astringent causes contraction of tissues.

balsamic soothing.

biennial a plant whose life cycle is completed over two growing seasons; with seed formation at the end of the second year.

boiling point the maximum, constant temperature at which a liquid evaporates at a given pressure.

bract a modified leaf at the base of a flower; e.g. the flowers of clary sage have large bracts.

carminative relieves flatulence.

catalyst a substance that can alter the rate of a chemical reaction, which remains unaltered in mass and composition at the end of the reaction.

cephalic benefits the head and mind, stimulating to the thought processes.

cholagogue promotes bile flow by stimulating the gall bladder.

choleretic promotes the secretion of bile by the liver.

cicatrisant promotes healing by formation of scar tissue.

cohobation the process of redistilling the distillation water to recover the water-soluble components of the essential oil.

colation a coarse filtration process, where a liquid is strained through a coarse filter to remove extraneous, insoluble particulate matter.

colloidal solution a dispersion of ultra-fine particles in a liquid medium.

concrete an aromatic solid or semi-solid extract containing essential oil, waxes and pigments, obtained by solvent extraction of aromatic plant material.

condensation the change in state from gas/vapour to liquid or solid.

corps purified fat, e.g. suet or lard, used in enfleurage.

cytophylactic promotes healing and repair of tissue, encourages growth of skin cells.

decongestant relieves congestion, e.g. of sinuses, of the respiratory system.

depurative removes impurities from the blood (detoxifying).

diaphoretic increases perspiration, assists excretory function of the skin.

digestive aids the process of digestion.

distillate the product of distillation collected in the receiver of the still.

diuretic increases urination.

drupe a fleshy fruit that contains a 'stone' (the seed surrounded by a hard casing) e.g. cherry.

emmenagogue promotes menstruation.

emollient soothes and softens the skin.

enfleurage the process of absorbing the fragrance from fresh flowers of a single species into a purified fatty medium over a period of time.

essential oil an odorous, volatile product, obtained by a physical process, from a natural source of a single botanical species, which corresponds to that species in name and odour (Williams 2000).

evaporation the change in physical state from liquid to gas/vapour.

expectorant aids the expulsion of mucus from the respiratory tract.

expression a mechanical process of scarification, or compression, for obtaining the volatile oil from the flavedo of citrus fruits.

extract the soluble matter obtained from an aromatic plant, by washing with a solvent that is then recovered by vacuum distillation. Extracts include concretes, absolutes and resinoids.
exudate a resinous substance produced by the cambium of some woody plants; aromatic exudates include benzoin, frankincense and myrrh.
febrifuge reduces fever.
fraction a group of essential oil constituents that have similar volatility and boiling points.
genus *plural* genera; the taxonomic category between family and species.
glabrous a plant surface devoid of hairs or other projections.
glands (essential oil producing), glandular cells, glandular hairs: a group of one or more cells whose main function is to secrete a plants volatile oil, e.g. glandular trichomes common in the Lamiaceae, vittae or resin canals in the Umbelliferae, secretory cells in flower petals, secretory cavities in the citrus fruits, etc.
glaucus a plant surface with a blue/grey waxy bloom.
haemostatic an agent that helps stop bleeding.
headspace the space above the surface of a liquid, bounded by the surrounding container. Headspace analysis is the analysis of the vapour present in the headspace.
hepatic aids liver function, assisting in detoxification process.
hepatotoxic toxic to the liver.
hydrophilic denotes that the substance will dissolve in water.
hypertensive an agent that raises the blood pressure.
hypnotic induces sleep.
hypotensive an agent that reduces blood pressure.
infloresence a flowering system comprising more than one flower.
isolate a single chemical constituent separated from an essential oil.
lanceolate a leaf that is narrow and tapering at both ends.

latent heat of vaporisation the amount of heat required to vaporise a given mass of liquid at the boiling point. The same quantity of heat is given out by the same weight of vapour when it condenses, at the boiling point.
laxative promotes bowel movement.
lipophilic denotes that a substance is fat-soluble.
lymphatic stimulant assists the tissue-cleansing function of the lymphatic system.
maceration the process of soaking a known weight of matter in a known volume of solvent, in a closed vessel, over a given period of time, after which the suspension is filtered, the soluble portion of the matter having dissolved in the solvent. This solution may be standardised to a given strength. If the solvent is alcohol, the resultant liquid is known as a tincture.
monoecious female and male reproductive organs are separated in different floral structures on the same plant; decreases the chances of self fertilisation.
mucolytic reduces the thickness of mucus in the respiratory tract.
necrotic causes tissue damage and tissue death.
nematicide an agent that will kill worms (nematodes).
nephrotoxic toxic to the kidneys.
nervine nerve tonic, neurotonic, strengthens the nervous system.
neurotoxic toxic to the nervous system.
oleo-gum resin a plant exudate composed of water-soluble gum, resin and volatile oil.
oleoresin a plant exudate consisting of resin and volatile oil.
order a taxonomic category comprising a group of families, the Latin name of which culminates in -ales, e.g. Geraniales, Coniferales or -florae, e.g. Tubiflorae.
panicle a branching flowering structure.
parturient aids childbirth.

perennial a plant that lives for many years. Herbaceous perennials usually die back and survive underground over the winter; woody perennials are trees and shrubs whose woody tissues persist above ground – they may be deciduous (lose leaves in the winter) or evergreen.

petiole the stalk of a leaf.

phlebotonic tonic (strengthening, astringent) to the veins.

phototoxicity application of a photosensitising substance to the skin, followed by exposure to UV light – will result in skin damage, burning, and a condition known as berloque dermatitis if bergaptene (in bergamot oil) is the agent.

polar a molecule that has separate regions with distinct positive and negative electrical charges; and that is usually water-soluble and fat-insoluble. Non-polar molecules tend to be the opposite.

pommade a product of the enfleurage process – a fragrance-saturated fat.

prophylactic prevents disease or infection.

racemose individual flowers are formed on individual stalks on the main axis.

receiver the vessel that collects the distillate from the condenser outlet.

rectification a process of redistillation of an essential oil to eliminate unwanted constituents, or to standardise the product.

resinoid the product of solvent extraction of an oleo-gum resin or an oleoresin, which contains the odorous constituents.

rhizome an underground stem that grows horizontally, and through branching allows vegetative propagation. Some are fleshy, allowing the storage of nutrients for over-wintering.

rubefacient increases local blood circulation causing redness of the affected area.

sedative relaxing in effect, reduces activity, promotes sleep.

sessile without a stalk.
sialogogue promotes salivation.
solute the dissolved substance in a solution.
solvent extraction the separation of soluble matter from a natural source of plant material, oleo-gum resin or oleoresin, using a pure, volatile solvent. At the end of the process, the solvent is recovered by vacuum distillation, leaving behind the product containing the odorous portion of the material. The product is a concrete, which can be further treated to produce an absolute, or a resinoid, which in some cases may be distilled to produce a volatile oil.
soporific induces sleep.
spasmogenic induces spasm in muscle tissue.
spasmolytic reduces spasm in muscle tissue.
spike a racemose inflorescence on which the sessile flowers are borne on an elongated axis.
steam distillation a process of distillation in which steam, under pressure, is used to heat a charge in a still, and release and vaporise the volatile molecules. The volatile portion is then condensed back into liquid form and collected in a receiver vessel.
still note a vegetable (cabbage-like) note that may be present in freshly distilled essential oil, which can be eliminated by brief aeration.
stimulant an agent that temporarily increases the function of a system, e.g. circulatory stimulant, immunostimulant.
sublimation the physical change in state from solid to vapour/gas phase, without going through the liquid phase.
sudorific promotes perspiration.
surface tension the stretching force observed at the surface of a liquid.

tonic generally supportive and restorative.
uterine tonic to the uterus.
vacuum distillation fractional distillation under a vacuum, which reduces the temperature required for the charge to reach boiling point; this eliminates thermal stress.
vacuum stripping evaporation of the product of solvent extraction in a vacuum, to remove traces of solvent that remain in the product.
vapour a gas, under specific conditions where a slight increase of pressure, or decrease in temperature will result in condensation into the liquid phase.
vasoconstrictor causes narrowing of the blood vessels.
vasodilator causes dilation of the blood vessels.
vesicant irritating to the skin, causes burning and blistering.
viscosity the thickness of a liquid, the internal friction within a liquid substance that opposes its tendency to flow freely.
volatile descriptive of a substance that evaporates when exposed to air. The term also applies to the low boiling point constituents of natural aromatic materials, e.g. plant volatile oils.
volatility the rate at which a substance evaporates. The concept of volatility has led to the classification of essential oils and aromatic extracts as top, middle and base notes.
vulnerary promotes healing of damaged tissue.
water distillation a distillation process suitable for a limited range of aromatic materials, where boiling water is in direct contact with the charge in the still.

Therapeutic Index

The Circulatory System

Key essential oils for poor peripheral circulation

- black pepper
- cinnamon leaf
- *Eucalyptus globulus*
- ginger
- juniper berry
- rosemary
- sweet marjoram

Key essential oils for varicose veins

- cypress
- geranium
- lemon
- patchouli

Key essential oils for fluid retention/toxic accumulation

- coriander seed
- grapefruit
- juniper berry
- lemon
- sweet fennel

Key therapeutic actions

- astringent
- circulatory stimulant
- depurative

- diuretic
- haemostatic
- lymphatic stimulant
- phlebotonic
- rubefacient
- vasoconstrictor
- vasodilator

Massage can improve circulation locally, enhance the elimination of metabolic wastes in the tissues and reduce oedema and fluid retention

The Digestive System

Digestive problems can include indigestion, acidity, loss of appetite, dyspepsia, irritable bowel syndrome, constipation, diarrhoea, flatulence, colic, etc. Many digestive problems are stress related. The spice and citrus oils are especially useful, as are some of the herbal essential oils.

Key essential oils that support the digestive system include

- black pepper
- cardamom
- clary sage
- coriander seed
- ginger
- nutmeg
- orange, bitter and sweet
- peppermint
- rosemary

- spearmint
- sweet fennel
- sweet marjoram

Key therapeutic actions

- antispasmodic
- aperitif
- carminative
- cholagogue
- digestive
- hepatic
- stomachic

Massage can reduce stress. Abdominal massage may be appropriate, especially if constipation is a feature.

The Female Reproductive System

Premenstrual Syndrome

Key essential oils

- diuretic oils to reduce fluid retention e.g. sweet fennel, juniper berry
- oils reputed to influence hormone production ('oestrogenic') e.g. clary sage, sage, cypress, sweet fennel, geranium and rose
- oils to counteract irritability/depression and 'mood swings' include geranium, jasmine, rose, ylang ylang, and Roman chamomile

Massage manipulations are designed to help reduce fluid retention and sensations of 'bloating' and may be helpful, carried out with general stress reduction measures.

Amenorrhoea

Key essential oils

- chamomile (German and Roman)
- clary sage
- jasmine
- rose
- sage
- sweet fennel

Dysmenorrhoea

Key essential oils are analgesic and antispasmodic

- clary sage
- lavender
- sage
- sweet fennel
- sweet marjoram

Massage should be very light over the abdomen, though it may not be tolerated. Hot compresses can be prepared for symptomatic relief.

Menopause Problems

Key essential oils

- chamomile (German and Roman)
- clary sage
- cypress
- geranium
- jasmine
- peppermint
- rose
- sage
- sweet fennel
- ylang ylang

Hydrosols, e.g. sage, rose, lavender, geranium or mint, can be misted over the face and upper body to provide symptomatic relief of 'hot flushes'.

The Immune System

Immune system problems include recurrent minor infections, allergies, and chronic fatigue syndrome.

Key essential oils are

- cinnamon leaf
- clove bud
- *Eucalyptus globulus*
- *Eucalyptus radiata*
- laurel
- niaouli

- palmarosa
- peppermint
- *Ravensara aromatica*
- spike lavender
- tea tree
- thyme (linalool)
- thyme (Moroccan, *Thymus saturoides*)
- thyme (thymol)

Allergies (Schnaubelt 1999)
- myrtle water
- niaouli
- peppermint
- *Tanacetum annuum*

Key therapeutic properties (Schnaubelt 1995, 1999)
- antimicrobial
- antiviral
- immunostimulant

The Integumentary System

Skin problems are often stress related. If a skin problem manifests, local massage may be contraindicated.

Key essential oils include
- bergamot
- cypress
- frankincense
- geranium

- German chamomile
- *Helichrysum*
- lavender
- lemon
- lemongrass
- myrrh
- palmarosa
- patchouli
- rose
- sandalwood
- tea tree (including lemon-scented tea tree)
- thyme
- vetivert
- yarrow
- ylang ylang

Key therapeutic actions

- anti-inflammatory
- antipruritic
- antiseborrhoeic
- antiseptic (antibacterial and antifungal)
- cicatrisant
- sedative actions may be appropriate if stress and anxiety is a feature
- vulnerary

Carriers are very important when blending, especially when the condition of the skin is a major consideration.

The Mental, Emotional & Behavioural Systems

Key essential oils for each area are outlined below.

Stress and tension – general

- clary sage
- lavender
- neroli
- ylang ylang

Anxiety/irritability

- benzoin resinoid
- bergamot
- clary sage
- geranium
- jasmine
- mandarin
- neroli
- orange
- patchouli
- petitgrain
- rose
- sandalwood
- ylang ylang
- vetivert

Depression/negative outlook

- bergamot
- geranium
- jasmine
- lime
- melissa

- petitgrain
- rose
- rosewood
- sandalwood
- ylang ylang

Poor memory/mental fatigue
- basil
- cardamom
- *Eucalyptus* (1,8-cineole species)
- ginger
- peppermint
- rosemary

Insomnia
- chamomile (German and Roman)
- lavender (low doses)
- mandarin
- melissa
- neroli
- rose
- sandalwood
- vetivert

Lethargy
- basil
- black pepper
- cardamom
- clary sage
- *Eucalyptus* (cineole)
- ginger

- jasmine
- juniper berry
- rosemary

The Musculoskeletal System

Key essential oils for muscular tension and pain, and arthritic and rheumatic conditions

- basil
- black pepper
- clary sage
- clove bud
- *Eucalyptus globulus*
- ginger
- juniper berry
- lemongrass
- nutmeg
- plai
- Roman chamomile
- rosemary
- Scots pine
- sweet marjoram
- *Thymus vulgaris*
- true lavender

The selection will be modified and influenced by all presenting symptoms and the emotional state.

Key therapeutic actions

- analgesic

- anti-inflammatory
- antispasmodic
- circulatory stimulant
- depurative
- rubefacient
- sedative/stimulant

Massage can relieve pain, induce muscular relaxation and the state of connective tissues, enhance body awareness, improve circulation and enhance the elimination of metabolic wastes in the tissues.

If massage is contraindicated, compresses may be used. Aqueous solutions can be even more effective than oil-based formulae (Harris 2002).

The Nervous System

Pain is commonly encountered – including headaches, neuralgia, and sciatica.

Key essential oils

- basil (including methyl chavicol type)
- clove bud
- *Eucalyptus* (cineole types)
- lavender
- nutmeg
- peppermint
- rosemary
- sweet marjoram

Key therapeutic properties
- analgesic
- anti-inflammatory
- antispasmodic
- cephalic
- sedative

Massage is useful for stress reduction and relaxation. Specific techniques like compression, friction or acupressure can relieve pain. Some carrier oils, such as tamanu and St John's Wort herbal macerated oils, are also analgesics.

The Respiratory System

Respiratory disturbances include catarrh, sinus congestion, coughs (productive, unproductive and nervous), respiratory tract infections, colds and asthma. Some problems may be stress related, e.g. hyperventilation.

Herbal essential oils such as sweet marjoram, rosemary and sweet fennel might help respiratory problems. Expectorant oils include *Eucalyptus* species (*E. globulus*, *E. polybractea*, *E. smithii*), white camphor. Other useful oils are myrtle, *Ravensara aromatica* (indicated for asthma) and thyme (indicated if prone to respiratory tract infections).

Key essential oils that support the respiratory system
- Atlas cedarwood
- benzoin resinoid
- cajeput
- cypress

- *Eucalyptus* (1,8-cineole types)
- fir
- frankincense
- ginger
- hyssop
- *Inula graveolens*
- myrrh
- myrtle
- niaouli
- peppermint
- *Ravensara aromatica*
- sandalwood
- Scots pine
- spearmint
- spike lavender
- sweet marjoram
- thyme

Key therapeutic actions

- antiseptic
- antispasmodic
- antitussive
- balsamic
- expectorant
- mucolytic
- sedative actions may be appropriate if stress and anxiety is a feature

Massage can reduce stress and can help the individual become aware of his or her breathing patterns. Percussive manipulations can alleviate congestion.

The Urinary System

The most common problems directly affecting this system are urinary tract infections.

Key essential oils

- bergamot
- coriander seed
- cypress
- grapefruit
- juniper berry
- niaouli
- orange
- rose
- sandalwood
- sweet fennel
- tea tree
- thyme (thymol)

Key therapeutic properties

- antibacterial
- anti-inflammatory
- antipruritic
- depurative
- diuretic
- immunostimulant

Massage is useful for pain relief and stress reduction. Abdomen massage is beneficial.

Essential oils can be used in baths to help alleviate symptoms of discomfort and help prevent recurrence of infections.

Significant Chemical Families

A summary of the most significant chemical constituents in terms of their chemical familes can be found in the following tables. The sources used to compile these tables are Lawless (1992), *Les Cahiers de l'Aromatherapie* vols 1 and 2 (1996), and Williams (1996).

Table 61
Monoterpenes

Key Points	Examples	Characteristic essential oils
• 10 carbon atoms • Cyclic, acyclic, chains, bicyclic, bridged carbon frameworks • Molecular weight 136 • Low polarity • Common essential oil constituents • Comparatively high volatility	Camphene, *delta*-3-carene, *para*-cymene, *d*- and *l*-limonene, myrcene (the β-isomer), ocimene, α- and β-pinene, β-phellandrene, sabinene, α-terpinene, γ-terpinene, terpinolene. Note: 'dipentene' is the name given to a mixture of *d*- and *l*-limonene.	*Boswellia carteri*, *Citrus* spp. except *C. bergamia* (limonene), *Juniperus communis, Origanum majorana, Pinus* spp. (α- and β-pinene), *Piper nigrum*

Table 62
Monoterpenoid alcohols

Key Points	Examples	Characteristic essential oils
• 10 carbon atoms • Cyclic, acyclic, chains and bicyclic carbon frameworks • Hydroxyl functional group • Moderate to high volatility • High polarity • Very common essential oil constituents, derived from the hydrolysis of various monoterpenes, e.g., camphene → borneol, ocimene → linalool, sabinene → thujan-4-ol, γ-terpinene → terpinen-4-ol, limonene, menthol	Borneol, *d*- and *l*-citronellol, geraniol, lavandulol, linalool, menthol, nerol, α-, β- and γ-terpineol, terpinen-4-ol, thujan-4-ol	*Aniba rosaeodora* (linalool), *Cymbopogon martinii* (geraniol), *Pelargonium graveolens* (citronellol), *Mentha piperita* (menthol), *Melaleuca alternifolia* (terpinen-4-ol), *Melaleuca viridiflora* (α-terpineol)

Table 63
Monoterpenoid aldehydes

Key Points	Examples	Characteristic essential oils
• 10 carbon atoms • Cyclic, acyclic, chains, bicyclic and bridged carbon frameworks • Aldehyde functional group • Moderate to high volatility • High polarity • Common essential oil constituents – there are not as many aldehydes as alcohols, they occur as major constituents of a few oils and minor constituents in many oils • They are derived from primary alcohols such as nerol, geraniol and *iso*-geraniol, citronellol and lavandulol	Citral – a mixture of the isomers geranial (citral a) and neral (citral b), citronellal, cuminaldehyde, geranial, neral, perillaldehyde	*Cymbopogon citratus, C. nardus* (citral), *Eucalyptus citriodora* (citronellal), *Cuminum cyminum* (cuminaldehyde), *Melissa officinalis* (citral and citronellal)

Table 64
Monoterpenoid ketones

Key Points	Examples	Characteristic essential oils
• 10 carbon atoms • Cyclic, acyclic, bicyclic and chain carbon frameworks • Ketone functional group • Moderate to high volatility • High polarity • Common essential oil constituents (major constituents of a few oils and minor constituents in many oils) • Formed from monoterpenes, e.g. α-pinene → verbenone ←→ verbenol; and also from certain monoterpenoid (secondary) alcohols, e.g. borneol → borneone (camphor) • Ketones cannot be further oxygenated and do not give rise to other metabolites	α- and β-asarone, camphor, d- and l-carvone, cryptone, fenchone, α-ionone, α-, β- and γ-irone, *cis*-jasmone, menthone and *iso*-menthone, methyl amyl ketone, methyl heptenone, methyl nonyl ketone, α- and β-thujone, perilla ketone, pinocamphone and *iso*-pinocamphone, pinocarvone, piperitone, *d*-pulegone, santolinenone, verbenone	*Anethum graveolens* (carvone), *Artemisia vulgaris* (thujone), *Cinnamomum camphora* (camphor), *Foeniculum vulgare* var. *amara* (fenchone), *Hyssopus officinalis* (pinocamphone), *Iris pallida* (irones), *Mentha piperita* (menthone), *Mentha pulegium* (pulegone), *Salvia officinalis* (thujone), *Thuja occidentalis* (thujone), *Viola odorata* (α-ionone)

Table 65
Terpenoid esters

Key Points	Examples	Characteristic essential oils
• Reaction products of primary or tertiary alcohols and carboxylic acids. For example, tertiary alcohol linalool reacts with acetic acid to form the ester linalyl acetate and water • Cyclic, acyclic, and chain carbon frameworks • Ester functional group • High polarity, also lipophilic • Moderate to high volatility • Common essential oil constituents, which occur as major constituents of a few oils and minor constituents in many oils	*Iso*-amyl angelate, *iso*-butyl angelate, citronellyl acetate, citronellyl formate, geranyl acetate, lavandulyl acetate, linalyl acetate, linalyl propionate, menthyl acetate, neryl acetate, sabinyl acetate, terpinyl acetate, *iso*-amyl tiglate	*Anthemis nobilis* (angelates and tiglates), *Citrus bergamia* (linalyl acetate), *Helichrysum angustifolium* (neryl acetate), *Juniperus sabina* (sabinyl acetate), *Lavandula angustifolia* (linalyl acetate), *Salvia lavandulaefolia* (sabinyl acetate), *Salvia sclarea* (linalyl acetate)

Table 66
Monoterpenoid oxides

Key Points	Examples	Characteristic essential oils
• Oxide functional group integrated within a cyclic carbon framework • Few oxides exist, only one significant monoterpenoid oxide – 1,8-cineole • 1,8-cineole is widespread, occuring in many essential oils. It is sometimes called eucalyptol • Moderate to high volatility • 1,8-cineole is a dominant constituent in a few essential oils	1,8-cineole, 1,4-cineole, linalool oxide, rose oxide. Note: ascaridole is an unsaturated terpene peroxide. A peroxide is identified by two oxygen atoms in the link between two carbons.	Many *Eucalyptus* spp. e.g. *E. globulus* (1,8-cineole), *Melaleuca* spp. e.g. *M. viridiflora* (1,8-cineole); *Hyssopus officinalis* var. *decumbens* (linalool oxide)

Table 67
Monoterpenoid phenols

Key Points	Examples	Characteristic essential oils
• Hydroxyl functional group and a short chain attached to an aromatic ring • Polar • Only three monoterpenoid phenols occur in essential oils, mainly in plants from temperate regions • Powerful antibacterial activity, and irritant to skin and mucus membranes	Australol, carvacrol, thymol	*Satureja hortensis* and *S. montana* (carvacrol and thymol), *Thymus capitatus* (carvacrol), *Thymus vulgaris* (thymol and carvacrol chemotypes), *Oregano vulgaris* (carvacrol)

Table 68
Sesquiterpenes

Key Points	Examples	Characteristic essential oils
• 15 carbon atoms • Chain, monocyclic and bicyclic structures • Molecular weight 204 • Less volatile than monoterpenes • Low polarity • Common, but less so than monoterpenes • Derived from the intermediate farnesyl pyrophosphate	α-bisabolene, α-cadinene, α-caryophyllene, β-caryophyllene (humulene), α-cedrene, chamazulene, α- and β-copaene, farnesene, patchoulene, α- and β-santalene, α- and β-zingiberene	*Commiphora myrrha* (α-bisabolene), *Matricaria recutita (chamazulene), Piper nigrum* (caryophyllene), *Syzigium aromaticum* (α-caryophyllene), *Juniperus virginiana* (α-cedrene), *Pogostemon cablin* (patchoulene), *Santalum album* (α- and β-santalene), *Zingiber officinale* (α- and β-zingiberene)

Table 69
Diterpenoids

Key Points	Examples	Characteristic essential oils
• 20 carbon atoms • Not common constituents, as they are generally too large to distil over	Salviol Sclareol	*Salvia officinalis* *Salvia sclarea*

Table 70
Sesquiterpenoids

Key Points	Examples	Characteristic essential oils
• 15 carbon atoms • Chain, monocyclic and bicyclic structures • Derived from sesquiterpenes • Polar • Less volatile than monoterpenes • Fairly widespread, some oils contain significant levels	**Alcohols** α-bisabolol, carotol, cedrol, farnesol, paradisiol, patchoulol, α- and β-santalol, viridiflorol, vetiverol, zingiberol	*Citrus paradisi* (paradisiol), *Daucus carota* (carotol), *Juniperus virginiana* (cedrol), *Matricaria recutita* (α-bisabolol), *Melaleuca quinquenervia/viridiflora, 'MVQ',* (viridiflorol), *Pogostemon cablin* (patchoulol), *Santalum album* (α- and β-santalol), *Vetiveria zizanoides* (vetiverol), *Zingiber officinale* (α- and β-zingiberol)
• Sesquiterpenoids are larger molecules than mono-terpenenoids, the carbon framework is more complex; thus, the functional group influence is less dominant	**Oxides** Bisabolol oxide and bisabolone oxide, caryophyllene oxide.	*Matricaria recutita*
	Lactones Alantolactone, costuslactone	*Inula helenium* *Saussurea costus*
• Oxygenated derivatives of sesquiterpenes largely occur as alcohols, oxides and lactones (cyclic esters)		

Table 71
Phenylpropanoids

Key Points	Examples	Characteristic essential oils
• Formed via the phenylpropane pathway • Molecules have one (or more) aromatic rings • Polar	**Phenylpropanoid phenols** Eugenol and *iso*-eugenol, methyleugenol, *para*-cresol	*Syzigium aromaticum* (eugenol), *Cinnamomum zeylanicum* (leaf oil – eugenol), *Juniperus oxycedrus* (*para*-cresol), *Melaleuca bracteata* (methyl eugenol), *Pimenta dioica* and *P. racemosa* (eugenol)
• Phenylpropanoids are found as phenols, alcohols, esters, aldehydes and ethers	**Phenylpropanoid alcohols** Benzyl alcohol and phenylethanol	*Rosa centifolia, R. damascena*
• Bifunctional and polyfunctional molecules exist, which can make classification difficult. For example, vanillin has an aldehyde group, an hydroxyl group and an ether group	**Phenylpropanoid aldehydes** *Para*-anisaldehyde, benzaldehyde, cinnamaldehyde	*Prunus amygdalus var. amara* *Cinnamomum zeylanicum*
	vanillin	*Styrax benzoin* and *Vanilla planifolia*
	Phenylpropanoid esters Benzyl acetate, benzyl benzoate, eugenyl acetate, methyl benzoate, methyl salicylate	*Betula lenta* (methyl salicylate), *Cananga odorata var. genuina, Gardenia jasminoides, Gaultheria procumbens* (methyl salicylate), *Jasminum officinale, Polyanthes tuberosa*

Table 71 (continued)
Phenylpropanoids

Key Points	Examples	Characteristic essential oils
	Phenolic ethers *Trans*-anethole, dill apiol, parsley apiol, elemicin, estragole (methyl chavicol), chavicol, methyl-β-phenylethyl ether, methyl-*para*-cresol, myristicin, safrole and *iso*-safrole	*Anethum graveolens* (dill apiol), *Artemisia dracunculus* (estragole), *Cananga odorata* (methyl-*para*-cresol), *Canarium luzonicum* (elemicin), *Foeniculum vulgare var. dulce* (*trans*-anethole), *Illicium verum* (*trans*-anethole), *Myristica fragrans* (myristicin), *Ocimum basilicum* (estragole), *Petroselinium sativum* (parsley apiol and myristicin), *Pimpinella anisum* (*trans*-anethole), *Sassafras albidum* (safrole)

Table 72
Carboxylic acids

Key Points	Examples
• Functional group is the carboxyl group • Generally low volatility • Not common essential oil constituents, usually not dominant • May be found in resinoids • Aliphatic and aromatic structures	Alantic acid, anisic acid, benzoic acid, cinnamic acid, citronellic acid, hydrocyanic (prussic) acid, phenylacetic acid, valerenic acid

Table 73
Furanocoumarins

Key Points	Examples
• Belong to the large chemical family of coumarins – over 1,000 exist in nature • Coumarin itself is a cyclic ester (lactone) with the distinctive odour of new- mown hay • The related furanocoumarins are found in the botanical families Rutaceae and Apiaceae (Umbelliferae) • Sometimes called psoralens, after a derivative of the coumarins. • Non- volatile, too large too be distilled, thus found in cold pressed oils and absolutes • Some are phototoxic agents	Bergapten (5-methoxy psoralen, 5-MOP), bergaptol (non phototoxic), bergamottin (bergaptyl geranyl ether, questionable phototoxicity), citropten, oxypeucedanin, xanthotoxin

Table 74
Fatty aldehydes

Key Points	Examples
• Related to the naturally occurring fats • Found as minor and trace components of essential oils, notably citrus oils • Hydrocarbons with between 7 and 12 carbon atoms arranged in chains • They are readily oxidised to fatty acids (carboxylic acids), which have a very unpleasant odour	Octanal (aldehyde C8), nonanal (aldehyde C9), decanal (aldehyde C10)

Table 75
Nitrogen-containing compounds

Key Points	Examples
• The amine functional group • Amines occur as esters, derived from anthranilic acid • The imine functional group • Imines exist in a cyclic form • Not common essential oil constituents • Found in trace amounts • In pure form, they possess unpleasant, powerful fishy and faecal odours respectively	**Amines** The aromatic esters methyl anthranilate (*Citrus sinensis, C. limon, C. reticulata, C.aurantium* var. *amara* flos. (neroli), *Cananga odorata, Jasminum officinale*) and methyl N-methyl anthranilate (*C. reticulata*) **Imines** Indole (*Citrus aurantium* var. *amara* flos. (neroli) and *Jasminum officinale*)

Table 76
Sulphur-containing compounds

Key Points	Examples
• These occur as sulphides, disulphides, trisulphides and esters • Generally, the presence of sulphur in a compound imparts a powerful, diffusive, unpleasant odour • Trace amounts present in a few oils; more significant amounts found in some oils of the Liliaceae family, e.g. garlic (*Allium sativum* var. *sativum*) and onion (*Allium cepa*) essential oils	Allyl isithiocyanate, allylpropyl disulphide, dimethyl sulphide, dimethyl disulphide, diallyl disulphide, diallylthiosulphate, diisopropyl disulphide, 3, 4-dimethylthiophene, methyl allyl trisulphide, phenylethyl isothiocyanate

Table 77
Carrier oils in aromatherapy

Carrier oils	Characteristics and properties
Almond (AKA sweet almond)	Fairly thick, not rapidly absorbed. Moisturising and emollient; soothing, antipruritic.
Apricot kernel*	Light texture, readily absorbed. For dry and sensitive skin; emollient and antipruritic.
Avocado*	Fairly thick; good skin penetration and feel. Promotes cell regeneration; skin hydration, aging or postmenopausal skin, sun damage, inflammation.
Borage	Use at up to 10% with other carriers. Soothing, moisturising, regenerating, firming.
Camellia*	Light texture, readily absorbed, good slippage for massage. Skin restructuring and moisturising properties, helps reduce appearance of scars, or prevent scarring.
*Centella asiatica**	Dermatitis and the healing of superficial wounds – surgical wounds and burns. It may improve circulation. Stimulates skin regeneration and helps with loss of elasticity.
Coconut (several products, including fractionated, light)	Unrefined product is solid at cool temperature, gives good lubrication and leaves a slightly greasy film on the skin. The fractionated product is a slightly viscous liquid and has skin softening properties. Unrefined product has skin and hair coating properties; soothing, moisturising.
Comfrey	Anti-inflammatory, used for breaks and sprains.
Evening primrose	Unsuitable as a lubricant on its own, but useful in combination with other carriers at up to 20%. Treament of eczema, psoriasis. Useful on dry skin. May improve skin elasticity and accelerate healing.

Table 77 (continued)
Carrier oils in aromatherapy

Carrier oils	Characteristics
Grapeseed	Good slippage. Prevents moisture loss, emollient.
Hazelnut*	Good lubricant, very good penetration and skin feel. Nourishing to the skin, slightly astringent, stimulates circulation. Emollient, restructuring properties and also prevents dehydration.
Jojoba*	Very compatible with skin, temperature sensitive (wax when cold), good slippage/skin feel. Protective, anti-inflammatory. Treatment for eczema, dandruff, sun damage and acne.
Kukui nut*	Very well absorbed and excellent skin feel. Possibly one of the most useful carriers. Treatment of superficial skin injuries and burns, slows down moisture loss, emollient (treatment of psoriasis and eczema). Antipruritic. Also used in cancer care (radiation treatment). Possibly even anti-aging.
Lime blossom	Used on wrinkles; emollient and antipruritic.
Macadamia nut*	Good penetration and slippage. Nourishing, moisturising, restructuring. Useful on mature skin.
Marigold* (*Calendula officinalis*)	Anti-inflammatory and vulnerary. Can be used for broken capillaries, varicose veins, bruises, eczema.
Olive	Heavy and sticky, pronounced odour. Soothing, anti-inflammatory and emollient – used on burns, sprains, bruises, dermatitis and insect bites.
Passion flower/seed	Light texture, readily absorbed, not greasy. Moisturising and emollient. Anti-inflammatory, treatment of burns. Relaxing.

* denotes particularly useful oil

Table 77 (continued)
Carrier oils in aromatherapy

Carrier oils	Characteristics
Peach kernel*	Light texture, but more body than Apricot kernel oil. Moisturising, skin regeneration, 'anti-aging'. Skin protection, antipruritic.
Rosehip seed oil	Too rich for massage but good in combination at 10–50%. Skin and tissue regeneration, may help scarring, burns, wounds and eczema. Also improves skin texture and discolouration. Useful on wrinkles.
Safflower	Inexpensive, light, but does not store well. Emollient.
Sesame	Sticky skin feel, however suitable in combinations at up to 20%. Skin restructuring, moisturising and emollient. Improves resilience and skin integrity.
St John's Wort*	Anti-inflammatory. Used for nerve pain, e.g. sciatica, neuralgia; on bruises and cuts; spasms. (Avoid sun).
Sunflower	Sticky skin feel, but reasonable slippage. Emollient.
Tamanu	Thick, sticky, strong odour, so not for massage unless in combination or as topical application. Relief of pain of shingles (50:50 with Ravensara aromatica). Healing and protective; analgesic, anti-inflammatory and cicatrisant. Increases local blood circulation.
Walnut*	Excellent, medium weight, good texture and skin feel for massage, fairly slow rate of absorption. Highly emollient reduces moisture loss, regenerative and anti-aging qualities. Treatment of eczema.
Wheatgerm	Thick, sticky, strong odour, not suitable for massage unless with other carriers at 5-10%. Anti-oxidant and emollient. Useful for mature or damaged skins.
Wild carrot	Tonic, cicatrisant and antipruritic. Treatment of eczema and psoriasis.

References

Arctander, S. (1960) *Perfume and Flavour Materials of Natural Origin*, Steffen Arctander, Elizabeth NJ. Cited in Lawless, J. (1992) *The Encyclopaedia of Essential Oils*, Element Books, Shaftesbury

Baerheim Svendsen, A. and J. J. C. Scheffer (eds) (1985) *Essential Oils and Aromatic Plants, Proceedings of the 15th International Symposium on Essential Oils*, Martinus Nijhoff/Dr W. Junk Publishers, The Netherlands

Balacs, T. (1997) 'Cineole-rich Eucalyptus', *International Journal of Aromatherapy*, vol. 8, no. 2, pp. 15–21

Bartram, T. (1995) *Encyclopaedia of Herbal Medicine*, Grace, Christchurch. Cited in Price, S. and L. Price (1999) *Aromatherapy for Health Professionals*, 2nd edition, Churchill Livingstone, Edinburgh

Beckstrom-Sternberg, S. M. and J. A. Duke (1996) *CRC Handbook of Medicinal Mints*, CRC Press, Boca Raton. Cited in Price, S. and L. Price (1999) *Aromatherapy for Health Professionals*, 2nd edition, Churchill Livingstone, Edinburgh

Bowles, E. J. (2003) *The Chemistry of Aromatherapeutic Oils*, 3rd edition, Allen & Unwin, Australia

Brud, W. S. and I. Ogyanov (1995) Zdravetz *International Journal of Aromatherapy*, vol. 7, no. 1, pp. 10–11

Brudnak, M. (2000) 'Cancer-Preventing Properties of Essential Oil Monoterpenes D-Limonene and Perillyl Alcohol', *Positive Health*, 2000, pp. 23–25

Buchbauer, G. (1993) 'Biological Effects and Modes of Action of Essential Oils', *International Journal of Aromatherapy*, vol. 5, no. 1, pp. 11–14

Buchbauer, G. (1996) Methods in Aromatherapy Research *Perfumer and Flavorist*, no. 21, pp. 31–36
Buchbauer, G., L. Jirovetz, W. Jager, J. Ilmeberger, and H. Dietrich (1993) in Teranchi *et al* (eds) *Bioactive volatile compounds from plants* (ACS Symposium Series), p. 525. Cited in Price, S. and L. Price (1999) *Aromatherapy for Health Professionals*, 2nd edition, Churchill Livingstone, Edinburgh
Buchbauer, G., W. Jager, L. Jirovetz, H. Dietrich and C. Plank (1991) *Zeitschrift Naturforschaft*, no. 46, pp. 1067–1072. Cited in Bowles, E. J. (2003) *The Chemistry of Aromatherapeutic Oils*, Allen & Unwin, Australia
Budhiraja, S. S., M. E. Cullum, S. S. Sioutis, L. Evangelista and S. T. Habanova (1999) 'Biological activity of Melaleuca alternifolia (tea tree) oil component, terpinen-4-ol, in human myelocytic cell line HL-60', *Journal of Manipulative Physiological Therapies*, vol. 22, no. 7, pp. 47–53. Cited in Bowles, E. J. (2003) *The Chemistry of Aromatherapeutic Oils*, Allen & Unwin, Australia
Caelli, M., J. Porteus, C. F. Carson, R. Heller and T. V. Riley (2001) 'Tea tree oil as an alternative topical decolonisation agent for Methicillin-resistant Staphylococcus aureus', *International Journal of Aromatherapy*, vol. 11, no. 2. pp. 97–99
Carson, C. F., B. D. Cookson, H. D. Farrelly and T. V. Riley (1995) 'Susceptibility of methicillin-resistant Staphylococcus aureus to the essential oil of Melaleuca alternifolia', *Journal of Antimicrobial Chemotherapy*, no. 35, pp. 421–424. Cited in Price, S. and L. Price (1999) *Aromatherapy for Health Professionals*, 2nd edition, Churchill Livingstone, Edinburgh
Carson, C. F., K. A. Hammer and T. V. Riley (1995) 'Broth microdilution method for determining the susceptibility of Escherichia coli and Staphylococcus aureus to the essential oil of Melaleuca alternifolia (tea tree oil)', *Microbios*, vol. 82, no.

332, pp. 181–185. Cited in Price, S. and L. Price (1999) *Aromatherapy for Health Professionals*, 2nd edition, Churchill Livingstone, Edinburgh

Carson, C. F. and T. V. Riley (1995) 'Antimicrobial activity of the major components of the essential oil of Melaleuca alternifolia', *Journal of Applied Bacteriology*, vol. 78, no. 3, pp. 264–269. Cited by Bowles, E. J. (2003) *The Chemistry of Aromatherapeutic Oils*, Allen & Unwin, Australia

Cavalieri, E., S. Mariotto, C. Fabrizi, A. C. de Prati, R. Gottardo, S. Leone, L. V. Berra, G. M. Lauro, A. R. Ciampa and H. Suzuki (2004) 'α-bisabolol, a non-toxic natural compound, strongly induces apoptosis in glioma cells', *Biochemical and Biophysical Research Communications*, no. 315 (2004), pp. 589–594

Clerc, O. (1995) 'Portraits in oils', *International Journal of Aromatherapy*, vol. 7, no. 1, pp. 15–17

Duraffourd, P. (1982) *En form tous les jours* Perigny: La Vie Claire cited in Price, S. and L. Price (2007) *Aromatherapy for Health Professionals*, 2nd edition, Churchill Livingstone, Edinburgh

Erligmann, A. (2001) 'Sandalwood oils' in *International Journal of Aromatherapy*, vol. 11, no. 4, pp. 186-192

Franchomme, P. (1985) *Phytoguide 1*, International Phytomedical Foundation, La Courtête. Cited in Lawless, J. (1992) *The Encyclopaedia of Essential Oils*, Element Books, Shaftesbury

Franchomme, P. and D. Pénoël (1990) *L'aromathérapie exactement*, Jallois, Limoges

Franchomme, P. and D. Pénoël (1990) *L'aromathérapie exactement*, Jallois, Limoges. Cited in Bowles, E. J. (2003) *The Chemistry of Aromatherapeutic Oils*, Allen & Unwin, Australia

Gimelli, S. P. (2001) *Aroma Science*, Micelle Press, Weymouth

Harris, R. (2002) 'Synergism in the essential oil world', *International Journal of Aromatherapy*, vol. 12, no. 4, pp. 179–186

Harris, B. (2005) 'Research Reports', *International Journal of Aromatherapy*, vol. 15, no. 4, pp. 207–210

Hirsch, A. R., Ye, Y., Lu, Y., Choe, M. (2007) 'The effects of the aroma of jasmine on bowling score', *International Journal of Essential Oil Therapeutics*, no. 1, pp. 79–82

Holmes (1994/1995) 'Sandalwood: the wisdom of being', *International Journal of Aromatherapy*, vol. 6, no. 4, pp. 14-17

Holmes, P. (1997) 'Fragrance Energetics: A Working Model of Holistic Aromapharmacology', *Aroma '97 Seminar Presentation* (Warwick University), Aromatherapy Publications, Brighton

Holmes, P. (1998) 'Jasmine – queen of the night', *International Journal of Aromatherapy*, vol. 8, no. 4, pp. 8–12

Hongratanaworakit, T. and G. Buchbauer (2007) 'Autonomic and emotional responses after transdermal absorption of sweet orange oil in humans: placebo controlled trial', *International Journal of Essential Oil Therapeutics*, no. 1, pp. 29–34

Jellinek, J. S. (1994) 'Aroma-Chology: A Status Review', *Perfumer and Flavourist*, vol. 19, pp. 25-48

Jouhar, A. J. (ed.) (1991) *Poucher's Perfumes, Cosmetics and Soaps Volume 1: The Raw Materials of Perfumery*, 9th edition, Chapman and Hall, London

Kerr, J. (1997) 'Essential oil profile – ylang ylang', *Aromatherapy Today*, no. 4, pp. 10–12

Kerr, J. (1998) 'Essential oil profile – chamomile', *Aromatherapy Today*, no. 6, pp. 10–15

Kirk-Smith, M. (1995) 'The Physiological and Psychological Effects of Fragrances', *Kingston-upon-Hull: ISPA Conference Proceedings*, ISPA, Leicester

Klimes, I. and D. Lamparsky (1976) Vanilla volatiles – a comprehensive analysis', *International Flavours Food and Additives*, no. 7, pp. 272–291

Knasko, S. C. (1997) 'Ambient odour: effects on human behaviour', *International Journal of Aromatherapy*, vol. 8, no. 3, pp. 28-33
Lavabre, M. (1990) *Aromatherapy Workbook*, Healing Arts Press, Vermont
Lawless, J. (1992) *The Encyclopaedia of Essential Oils*, Element Books, Shaftesbury
Lawless, J. (1995) *The Encyclopaedia of Essential Oils*, Element Books, Shaftesbury
Lawless, J. (1996) *The Encyclopaedia of Essential Oils*, Element Books, Shaftesbury
Lawrence, B. (1979) *Essential Oils 1976–1978*, Allured Publishing Corporation, Illinois
Leffingwell, J. C. (2000) 'Osmanthus', Leffingwell and Associates, retrieved from: www.leffingwell.com
Lind, E. M. (1998) 'Profile of tuberose', *Aromatherapy Quarterly*, no. 56, pp. 17–20
Lis-Balchin, M. (1995) *The Chemistry and Bioactivity of Essential Oils*, Amberwood Publishing Ltd, Surrey
Lis-Balchin, M. (1996) 'Geranium oil', *International Journal of Aromatherapy*, vol. 7, no. 3, pp. 18–20
Mailhebiau, P. (1995) *Portraits in Oils*, C. W. Daniel Co. Ltd, Saffron Walden
Mailhebiau, P., P. Goëb and J. Azémar (1996) 'Properties and indications: Rosmarinus officinalis', *Aromatherapy Records*, no. 2, pp. 40–45
Maury, M. (1989) *Marguerite Maury's Guide to Aromatherapy – the secret of life and youth: a modern alchemy*, C. W. Daniel Co. Ltd, Saffron Walden
Mertz, D. F. (1994) 'New Zealand Coromandel Mountains', Tea Tree Oil Company, Whitianga: unpublished report
Mills, S. Y. (1991) *The Essential Book of Herbal Medicine*, Penguin

Arkada, Harmondsworth. Cited in Price, S. and L. Price (2007) *Aromatherapy for Health Professionals*, 2nd edition, Churchill Livingstone, Edinburgh

Mojay, G. (1996) *Aromatherapy for Healing the Spirit*, Gaia Books, London

Mojay, G. (1998) 'Aromatic acupressure – the therapeutic application of specific essential oils for the organ meridians and acupressure points of oriental medicine', *International Journal of Aromatherapy*, vol. 9, no. 3, pp. 105–114

Mojay, G. (1999) *Aromatic Energetics and the Oriental Five Elements*, Institute of Traditional Herbal Medicine and Aromatherapy, London

Morris N., Birtwistle S., Toms, M. (1995) 'Anxiety Reduction', *International Journal of Aromatherapy*, vol. 7, no. 2, pp. 33–39

Pénoël, D. (1991) *Médecine aromatique, médecine planétaire*, Jallois, Limoges. Cited in Price, S. and L. Price (1999) *Aromatherapy for Health Professionals*, 2nd edition, Churchill Livingstone, Edinburgh

Pénoël, D. (1992) 'Winter Shield', *International Journal of Aromatherapy*, vol. 4, no. 4. pp. 10–12

Pénoël, D. (1998/1999) 'Medical aromatherapy', *International Journal of Aromatherapy*, vol. 9, no. 4, pp. 162–165

Pongprayoon, U. (1997) 'Topical anti-inflammatory activity of the major lipophilic constituents of zingiber cassumunar', *Part 1: The Essential Oil Phytomedicine*, vol. 3, no. 4, pp. 319–322

Price, L. (1998) 'Oils from the Myrtaceae family', *Aromatherapy World*, harvesting issue

Price, S. and L. Price (1999) *Aromatherapy for Health Professionals*, 2nd edition, Churchill Livingstone, Edinburgh

Price, S. and L. Price (2007) *Aromatherapy for Health Professionals*, 3rd edition, Churchill Livingstone, Edinburgh

Reynolds, J. E. F. (ed.) (1972) *Martindale: the extra pharmacopoeia*, 29th edition, Pharmaceutical Press, London. Cited in Price, S. and L. Price (1999) *Aromatherapy for Health Professionals*, 2nd edition, Churchill Livingstone, Edinburgh

Rose, J. (1999) *375 Essential Oils and Hydrosols*, Frog Ltd, Berkeley

Safayhi, H., J. Sabieraj, E. R. Sailer and H. P. Ammon (1994) 'Chamazulene: an antioxidant-type inhibitor of leukotriene B4 formation', *Planta Medica*, vol. 60, no. 5, pp. 410-413. Cited in Bowles, E.J. (2003) *The Chemistry of Aromatherapeutic Oils*, 3rd edition, Allen & Unwin, Australia

Santana, A., S. Ohashi, L. de Rosa (FCAP) and C. L. Green (1997) 'Brazilian rosewood oil', *International Journal of Aromatherapy*, vol. 8, no. 3, pp. 16-20

Schnaubelt, K. (1995) *Advanced Aromatherapy*, Healing Arts Press, Vermont

Schnaubelt, K. (1998) *Advanced Aromatherapy – the science of essential oil therapy*, Healing Arts Press, Vermont

Schnaubelt, K. (1999) *Medical Aromatherapy – healing with essential oils*, Frog Ltd, Berkeley

Schnaubelt, K. (2000) 'Functional group therapy', *International Journal of Aromatherapy*, no. 10 (1/2), pp. 62–63

Schnaubelt, K. (2003) 'Theory and practice in aromatherapy', *In Essence*, vol. 2, no. 1, pp. 8-10

Sheen, J. and J. Stevens (2001) 'Self perceived effects of sandalwood', *International Journal of Aromatherapy*, vol. 11, no. 4, pp. 213-219

Shen, J., A Niijima, M. Tanida, Y. Horii, K. Maeda and K. Nagai (2005) 'Olfactory stimulation with scent of grapefruit oil affects autonomic nerves, lipolysis and appetite in rats', *Neuroscience Letters*, no. 380, pp. 289–294. Cited in Harris, B. (2005) 'Research Reports', *International Journal of Aromatherapy*, vol. 15, no. 4, pp. 207–210

Sorensen, J. M. (2000) 'Melissa officinalis', *International Journal of Aromatherapy*, no. 10 (1/2), pp. 7–15
Soulier, J-M. (1995) 'The Thymus genus', *Aromatherapy Records*, no. 1, pp. 38–56
Soulier, J-M. (1996) 'The Rosmarinus genus', *Aromatherapy Records*, no. 2, pp. 29–35
Tester-Dalderup, C. B. M. (1980) 'Drugs used in bronchial asthma and cough', Dukes, M. N. G. (ed.) *Meyler's Side Effects of Drugs*, 9th edition, Excerpta Medica, Amsterdam. Cited in Price, S. and L. Price (1999) *Aromatherapy for Health Professionals*, 2nd edition, Churchill Livingstone, Edinburgh
The International School of Aromatherapy (1993) *A Safety Guide on the Use of Essential Oils*, Natural by Nature Oils Ltd, London
Tisserand, R. and T. Balacs (1994) 'Nutmeg', *International Journal of Aromatherapy*, vol. 6, no. 4, pp. 28–38
Tisserand, R. and T. Balacs (1995) *Essential Oil Safety – A Guide for Health Care Professionals*, Churchill Livingstone, London
Torii, S. (1997) 'Odour mechanisms: the psychological benefits of odour', *International Journal of Aromatherapy*, vol. 8, no. 3, pp. 34–39
Turin, L. (1996) 'A spectroscopic mechanism for primary olfactory reception', *Chemical Senses*, no. 21, pp. 773–791
Valder, C., Neugbauer, M., Meier, M., Kohlenberg, B. (2003) 'Western Australian sandalwood oil – new constituents of *Santalum spicatum* (R. Br.) A. DC. (Santalaceae)', *Journal of Essential Oil Research*, May/June 2003
Van der Walt (1977 and 1985) cited in Weiss, E. A. (1997) *Essential Oil Crops*, CAB International, Wallingford
Van Toller, S and G. H. Dodd, eds (1988) *Perfumery, the Psychology and Biology of Fragrance*, Chapman and Hall, London
Warren, C. and S. Warrenburg (1993) 'Mood benefits of fragrance',

International Journal of Aromatherapy, vol. 5, no. 2, pp. 12–16
Weiss, E. A. (1997) *Essential Oil Crops*, CAB International, Wallingford
Weiss, E. A. (2002) *Spice Crops*, CAB International, Wallingford
Wells, C. (2002) 'Plai', *Essentially Oils Newsletter*, March 2002, Essentially Oils, Oxfordshire
Whitton, S. (1994) 'Yarrow', *Aromatherapy Quarterly*, no. 40, pp. 14–17
Williams, D. G. (1996) *The Chemistry of Essential Oils*, Micelle Press, Dorset
Williams, D. G. (2000) *Lecture Notes on Essential Oils*, 2nd edition, Eve Taylor London Ltd, London
Williams, L. R., J. K. Stockley, W. Yan and V. N. Home (1998) 'Essential oils with high antimicrobial activity for therapeutic use', *International Journal of Aromatherapy*, vol. 8, no. 4, pp. 30–40

Essential Oils, Absolutes & Resinoids Index